DEC 1 0 2002

Digital Photography

99 easy tips
to make you look like a pro!

Digital Photography

99 easy tips

778.3
M

to make you look like a pro!

Ken Milburn

McGraw-Hill Osborne

New York   Chicago   San Francisco   Lisbon
London   Madrid   Mexico City   Milan   New Delhi
San Juan   Seoul   Singapore   Sydney   Toronto

McGraw-Hill/Osborne
2600 Tenth Street
Berkeley, California 94710
U.S.A.

To arrange bulk purchase discounts for sales promotions, premiums, or fund-raisers, please contact **McGraw-Hill/**Osborne at the above address. For information on translations or book distributors outside the U.S.A., please see the International Contact Information page immediately following the index of this book.

Digital Photography: 99 Easy Tips to Make You Look Like a Pro!

34567890 CUS CUS 0198765432

ISBN 0-07-222582-3

Publisher:	Brandon A. Nordin
Vice President &	
Associate Publisher:	Scott Rogers
Acquisitions Editor:	Marjorie McAneny
Project Editor:	Janet Walden
Acquisitions Coordinator:	Tana Allen
Technical Editor:	Rowena White
Copy Editor:	Lisa Theobald
Proofreader:	Paul Tyler
Indexer:	David Heiret
Computer Designers:	Kelly Stanton-Scott, Jean Butterfield
Illustrators:	Lyssa Sieben-Wald, Michael Mueller
Series Design:	Mickey Galicia, Peter Hancik
Cover Design:	Pattie Lee

This book was composed with Corel VENTURA™ Publisher.

Dedication

I would like to dedicate this book to
Janine Warner, without whom
none of this would have
happened.

About the Author

Ken Milburn started taking pictures the year he entered high school and was working professionally as a wedding photographer by the time he graduated. He has been involved with photography both as a hobby and professionally ever since, and he has worked in advertising, travel, and fashion photography. He has been working with computers since 1981 and has written hundreds of articles, columns, and reviews for such publications as *Publish*, *DV* magazine, *Computer Graphics World*, *PC World*, *Macworld*, and *Windows* magazine. He has published 10 other computer books, including the first edition of *The Digital Photography Bible*, *Master Visually Photoshop 6*, *Master Photoshop 5.5 VISUALLY*, *Cliff's Notes on Taking and Printing Digital Photos*, and *Photoshop 5.5 Professional Results*. Ken also maintains a practice as a commercial photo-illustrator and has become internationally known for his photopaintings, which have been featured twice in *Design Graphics* magazine, in the all-time best-selling poster for the 1998 Sausalito Arts Festival, and in the 1999 American President Lines calendar.

Contents at a Glance

Contents

Acknowledgments

If it weren't for Gene Hirsh, my friend and the co-author of our *Photoshop Elements: The Complete Reference*, it is unlikely that this book would have made it to press on time. When illness and deadline pressures from other projects got to me, Gene gave it his all to make sure that the project happened. Gene, you're the man. Thank you and God bless.

I also want to thank my brilliant and charming acquisitions editor for her persistent calm, sense of humor, and practical approach to life. Margie McAneny belongs in the top rung of acquisitions editors. Tana Allen is equally diligent and conscientious, not to mention great to work with. I also want to extend a warm thanks to Rowena White, Janet Walden, and Lisa Theobald for their skillful editing. Bravo to Peter Hancik for a great design and also to Pattie Lee for an eye-catching cover. Finally, I extend big thank you to my long-time agent, Margot Maley Hutchinson, for all her work in making this project a reality.

Lots of companies helped us out with review copies of their software and with review units of their cameras. You'll see photographs and mentions of these products throughout the book. Copious thanks to all of these companies for their help! Without it, we wouldn't have been able to gather nearly as much valuable information. I'd also like to make special mention of Nikon and Olympus; both companies made sure we were kept up-to-date and were especially quick to respond to our needs. And special thanks also to the people at TechSmith for the constant updates to SnagIt! (which created all of the screenshots in this book) and Camtasia, a program that's great at capturing the screen in motion.

Introduction

You've done it! You finally went out and bought that digital camera you've heard so much about and now you're staring at it, wondering how to make the thing work. It can be a bit intimidating at first. Do you find yourself pondering all those buttons, screens, and dials and scratching your head? Where do you put in the film anyway? It's OK, though, because you did one thing right. You purchased this book, which places you firmly on the path to shooting digital photographs like a pro.

This book was conceived with the novice digital photographer in mind. For that reason, I have kept the language in plain English; where technical terms are used, they include a clear, concise, no-nonsense explanation. The digital camera is complex enough without making you learn a whole new technical language. So rest assured that this book will make your life a bit easier by demystifying the subject as much as possible, making it possible for you to easily grasp this content and make it work for you.

Much of the knowledge in this user-friendly book was gained over my years of hard-knocks experience. The 99 tips herein will help you take control of your camera, compose better photos, and will then launch you into the power of digital editing.

My hope is that you will find this book a helpful companion in introducing you to the tools and techniques that pros use to get dramatic results. The only difference between an amateur and a pro is knowledge and experience. I plan to convey to you the essential knowledge that will make the experience a rewarding one and start you on your way to more accomplished work.

Digital photography is a new invention, so practically everyone is a novice—or was one not so long ago. I wanted to mention this so you will feel comfortable and encouraged in your pursuit of this fascinating new aspect of photography. You have lots of company in this pursuit, because we are all, even the pros, learning what digital photography can do. Think of this as the "Digital Photography Gold Rush"—you, too, can stake out your claim!

I have worked hard to devise a format for this book that will be easy to use. The information presented in the tips follows a general structure of *what* is it?, *why* do you need it?, and *how* do you do it? This allows you to get at the information you want quickly, without having to sift through pages of text. I think you will find this a useful guide to stash in your camera case and to use for reference again and again. I wish I had this book when I started out. Perhaps that's why I wrote it.

I have chosen to use Adobe Photshop Elements to demonstrate many of the image-editing techniques in this book, because I feel it is one of the most robust image editors to hit the market at a low price. Adobe Photoshop Elements was fashioned after Adobe Photoshop, a professional-level image editor. By using Elements, which actually shares many of the same features as Adobe Photoshop, you can get a good sense of and feel for what professionals use everyday. If you want to try out Adobe Photoshop Elements, you can download a free demo version at http://www.adobe.com/products/photoshopel/.

Make This a Better Book: Talk to the Author

I may not be able to answer all the e-mail I get, but I'll certainly read them and your voice will have an influence on future editions. Unfortunately, if I'm up against paying deadlines when you write, it may not be practical to get back to you right away. Please don't let that discourage you from letting me know what you think—especially if you have constructive suggestions for improving this book. Immediately following the completion of this book, my Web site was thoroughly redesigned. One of the new features is a gallery of photos with "How I Did It" tips attached. Watch the site for frequent updates and news and reviews of breaking developments in the digital photography field. My Web site address is http://www.kenmilburn.com. You can reach my e-mail address through the Web site.

–Ken Milburn

Part I

Taking Full Advantage of Your Camera

Chapter 1

How Does a Digital Camera Work?

Anyone, and that includes professionals, who first picks up a digital camera can be a bit intimidated—all those new buttons, screens, and dials. I am here to demystify the device so you harness the power the digital camera gives you. Understanding how a digital camera works at the functional level establishes the foundation you need to take good photographs. The camera is your tool in capturing your vision and, as any craftsman will tell you, knowing your tools is key to creating high-quality work. In this chapter, I will go over all the parts of the camera, explain their functions, and familiarize you with their unique features and terminology.

1. The Basic Parts of a Digital Camera

First, you must get familiar with the basic components of a digital camera, which have many features that you won't find on conventional cameras and some that you will. Figure 1-1 illustrates the typical location and configuration of the components on most digital cameras. Your camera may vary in the exact location, so also refer to your manual if you need further clarification.

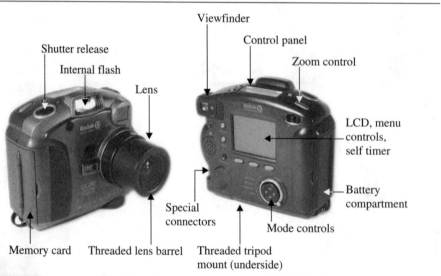

FIGURE 1-1   Components of the digital camera

Battery Compartment

This is the slot where you install your camera's batteries. The batteries may be rechargeable or standard types and come in various sizes. Most digital cameras hold multiple batteries.

Control Panel

The control panel is "information central." This is a small LCD display, usually located on the top of the camera or on the topside of the back of the camera, that displays the current settings, battery life, number of images remaining to be taken, and mode operation of the camera. The symbols and items displayed vary with different manufactures, but these are slowly becoming standardized.

Internal Flash

The internal flash is a built-in electronic strobe-type flash that is timed to go off with the release of the shutter. It can also be suppressed, forced, or delayed via menu controls for various shooting conditions (see Chapter 5).

LCD

LCD stands for *liquid crystal display*. This is a reference to the type of technology that was used in the early flat-panel video displays. Many technologies are used now, but LCD has become a generic term for a flat video display. Think of it as a small television screen on the back of your camera and sometimes in the viewfinder. It displays what the lens "sees" (as opposed to the slightly offset and distorted view that an optical viewfinder provides), shows previews of the shots that you have taken, and displays the camera's interactive menus in color. You can even see motion video on the LCD—if your camera supports that feature.

Lens

The lens is a piece of ground glass or plastic that focuses the light on the sensors. It is mounted in a cylindrical housing, which is attached to the front of the camera. The lens (or some of the elements within it) moves within the housing closer or nearer to the image sensors, which allows the image to focus. Some lenses are permanently mounted to the camera and others are detachable and interchangeable. The lens is your primary eye on the world in photography, so lens quality is very important. A significant portion of what you pay for in a camera should be due to the quality of the optics.

Mode Controls

Mode controls can be in the form of dials or buttons on the top or back of the camera. They allow you to switch between various basic shooting modes so that your camera can be made to adapt quickly to the conditions of the shoot. Examples of such mode controls are programmed or automatic, aperture-priority, and shutter-priority. Although many other types of mode settings are available, these choices vary wildly from one camera model to another. (See Chapter 3 for more information on modes.)

Menu Controls

You'll find the menu controls on the back of the camera, shown on the LCD in the form of an interactive video display. You can change a wide range of camera options using these controls.

Memory Card Compartment

The memory card compartment is a small door or slot in the side or on the bottom of the camera that allows for the insertion of a memory card or disk. Images are stored on the memory card. (See Tip 10 in Chapter 2 for more on memory cards.)

Viewfinder

The viewfinder is a small eyepiece located on the top part of the camera. Viewfinders come in three varieties—optical, electronic, and through-the-lens (see Tip 24 in Chapter 4). Viewfinders are designed to simulate what the lens is seeing to enable you to frame your picture.

Self Timer

The self timer allows you to set a timer so that you can walk away from the camera and have it take the photo after a short delay. A few digital cameras also come with wireless remote switches that can trigger the camera to take a photo from a distance. Self timers are often used in place of cable releases to keep the camera from jiggling and blurring the photo when the shutter release is pressed.

Shutter Release

The shutter release is a multifunction button, usually found on the top right part of the camera. It is used in its half-pressed mode to set metering and focus. In its fully pressed mode, it releases the shutter to expose the electronic image sensors and capture the image.

Special Connectors

Special connectors are extra outputs and inputs that allow for the attachment of external power, external flash, audio, video, and computer connections. Because not all cameras include all of these connections, you should shop carefully to make sure that those connections you need are included on the camera.

Threaded Lens Barrel

If the front of the lens barrel is threaded, it can accept a wide variety of color-balancing, special-effects, and close-up filters. It is also much more able to adapt to supplementary telephoto and wide-angle lenses. You can spot a threaded lens barrel by looking at the inside rim of the metal that surrounds the front lens element. If you see screw threads, obviously the barrel is threaded. Some cameras require you to push on nonthreaded adapters, increasing the chances that a supplementary lens could be accidentally knocked from its perch. Unthreaded barrels are most often found on cameras whose lenses retract into the camera body or on low-priced cameras.

Threaded Tripod Mount

The threaded mount is a bolt hole in the bottom of the camera that accepts the mounting screw for tripods, camera stands, external flash units, and other types of camera mounting hardware. The screw size and thread are nearly always one-quarter inch in diameter. Some larger, more expensive, and sturdier tripods and accessories use a one-third-inch mounting screw, but users of consumer-level digital cameras seldom need be concerned with these.

Zoom Control

If your camera has a zoom lens, it will have a control that widens or narrows the angle of view. The control, in the form of a toggle switch, is usually found on top of the camera. Zooming allows you to move closer to your subject without changing your position.

2. The Basic Differences Between Conventional and Digital Cameras

Even though conventional cameras have been including more and more electronic features, the primary operation of the camera is mechanical. To take a photograph, the shutter has to open to expose the film inside. Digital cameras have almost completely eliminated the mechanical aspect of photography. About the only place that moving parts still exist in digital cameras is in the focus and zoom functions of the lenses.

If you have operated a single-lens reflex (SLR) camera, you will find that using a digital camera is similar in a lot of ways. SLRs are typically 35mm film cameras that let you see directly through the lens via a mirror that reflects the image to the viewfinder. The mirror moves out of the way when the shot is taken.

The following is a comparison list pointing out some of the basic differences between digital and conventional cameras:

Digital Cameras	Conventional Cameras
Memory cards can be reused	Hand-loaded film—needs processing
Can view shots immediately on LCD	Have to wait for processing (except for Polaroid—60 sec.)
Can preview a catalog of shots in memory	No preview
Can take shots over again many times and not use more memory	No way to reuse film after it has been exposed
Low to good resolution	Good to excellent resolution
Can record motion sequences (some models)	Can't record video
Can record audio (some models)	Can't record audio
Batteries must be recharged often	Small batteries last a long time (except motor-drive cameras)
Swiveling LCD allows framing from odd angles (some models)	Need to frame through the viewfinder
Zoom lenses	Zoom lenses
Detachable lenses only on most expensive models	Detachable lenses on all but least expensive models
Few to no moving parts	Many moving parts

3. Know Your Resolution

Resolution in digital photography refers to the number of individual *pixels* (discrete picture elements) that are used to define the detail in the image. Think of pixels as tiny, solid-color square tiles in a very large mosaic tabletop picture. Image size is defined by pixel dimensions, as in 640×480, which refers to the number of horizontal (640) and vertical (480) pixels in the matrix that makes up the picture. The higher the resolution, the clearer and more detailed the picture appears.

Inside your digital camera are specialized light-sensitive chips, called *image sensors*. Image sensors use either Complementary Metal Oxide Semiconductor (CMOS) or Charge-Coupled Device (CCD) technology. (Ironically, only the newest and highest definition or the cheapest and lowest definition cameras currently use CMOS technology.) These chips are made up of arrays of image sensors. Each sensor translates the light falling on it into electronic signals, which define color and intensity. This information is stored as digital data in a computer data device that's built into the camera or as flash memory on a removable card. The data on these cards is translated by computer programs and displayed as color pixels on a computer screen or the camera's LCD.

Figure 1-2 shows the same image displayed at low resolution and high resolution. You can see how the pixels appear more "blended" at a higher resolution.

You will notice that each camera comes with a pixel rating, such as 1.3 megapixels (million pixels) or 3.2 megapixels on up to 6 megapixels in the newest models. More megapixels translate to more individual light sensors on the image chip, which translates to higher image definition, which translates to sharper, clearer pictures. Your camera's megapixel rating determines how much detail can be captured in the highest resolution setting. You can usually blow up standard 35mm film to 8×10, 11×14, and in some cases 16×20 without seeing too much loss in quality, but go any further and the quality starts to go downhill.

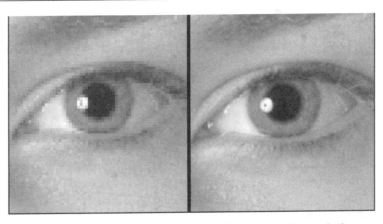

Resolution at 1 megapixel   Resolution at 3 megapixels

FIGURE 1-2   You can see the difference in image quality between low resolution (left) and high resolution (right) digital cameras.

With digital cameras, the resolution of the image sensor determines the detail, so if you want the ability to blow up your pictures to any great degree, you will need to use a higher resolution mode. The 5- and 6-megapixel digital cameras are the first to produce images with quality similar to that of film. Popularly priced 2-megapixel digital cameras will allow for passable inkjet or photographic prints of up to 8×10 in size, comparable to machine-made prints available from consumer-level one-hour photo labs.

On the other hand, if your image is targeted for online display, such as the Web, video, or animation, the need for resolution will be much lower. The best advice is to buy the highest capacity memory cards you can afford and shoot all your pictures at the highest resolution your camera will allow. You may think you have a good reason to shoot at a lower resolution, but the only really good reason is if you just have no other way to get the shots you want to take without running out of memory before you can download the images off the memory card and start over. After all, it's always better to have *some* picture of something that's important to you than no picture at all. It's equally important to remember that if detail and quality don't exist in the image you shoot, you are never going to be able to restore it later. Remember that you can never take exactly the same picture twice. (Well, almost never. Still-life photos taken under controlled studio lighting conditions are the one exception I can think of.)

Try This: Up Close and Personal with Pixels

If you have the ability to load your camera's images onto your computer, you might use your image-editing software to zoom in on a part of the image to get a closer look at the pixel structure. Try doing test shots of the same scene or object at various resolution settings to see the differences. If you can look at film under magnification, you will see the grain structure—and a lot of similarities between pixels and grain. Although film is often referred to as *continuous tone,* that is not factually correct. Film has discrete color elements that are similar to pixels. The big difference is that the film's elements have a random shape and size whereas digital pixels are uniform squares in a grid—with no empty space in between them. So, in a sense, digital images are grainless.

Why Is Resolution Important?

The more resolution (pixels) your camera can capture, the finer the detail in the photograph and the more information you have to work with later in editing or printing the image. Due to the rapid advancements in digital technology, today's digital cameras are approaching the quality of conventional film—and may soon surpass it. Higher resolution means sharper and more detailed pictures.

The resolution ultimately affects output (this applies to printers, film recorders, video, or the Web). Every type of output demands a certain amount of information from the images that it uses for input (the image stored on the memory card in pixels). Prints and slides demand a significantly larger number of pixels (about 240 to the printed inch) to produce good quality. (See Chapter 14.) Video and the Web require much less (between 72 pixels and 96 pixels to the displayed inch). (See Chapter 7.)

Cropping a part of a photo throws away pixels and, therefore, affects resolution. You can't replace that resolution if you then enlarge the cropped image. Understanding what your target output is going to be will help you choose the appropriate resolution settings and help you learn how to frame your image to maximize results. However, as I mentioned earlier, the simplest way to deal with this is to capture every image with as much resolution as your camera can accommodate.

How Do I Adjust Resolution?

Most cameras provide multiple resolution settings. You can access the menu for selecting the resolution options through your LCD menu options panel. The exact pixel dimensions of each resolution setting will vary according to the megapixel rating of the camera. It is a very good idea to keep the camera set at its highest quality, highest resolution setting until you have a critical need to capture more pictures than that setting will allow. Remember, once you've taken the picture, you can never increase its quality. Nor can you retake the picture.

NOTE
It's a good idea to check your camera's control panel after you change resolution settings to see how many shots you can store on your memory card. This will allow you to gauge your shoot.

The following table provides a comparison chart to indicate the range of output capabilities that are practical for the resolution rating of the camera. The higher resolution cameras give you the greatest range and flexibility.

Camera Resolution Ranges*	Up to 8×10 Prints	8×10–11×14 Prints	Poster-Sized Prints	Inkjet Prints	Web Graphics
1 megapixel range—very low 640×480 to 1024×768					x
2 megapixel range—low 1280×960	x			x	x
3 megapixel range—medium 1200×1600	x	x		x	x
4 megapixel range—high 2272×1704	x	x	x	x	x
5+ megapixel range—very high 3008×1960	x	x	x	x	x

*The resolutions indicated represent an average for the range in that category. Actual resolutions may vary somewhat according to manufacturer and model.

About Image Quality Settings

In addition to giving you a choice of resolution settings, most digital cameras let you choose what they call "image quality." Why provide two settings that seem to amount to the same thing? Because they are really two independent factors, each of which contributes to overall image quality. Resolution is one of these factors. The degree of "lossy" compression used in writing the file to JPEG (for Joint Photographic Experts Group) format is the other.

JPEG is the image file format that is most often used by digital cameras, because it saves space and allows you to record more images on the memory card. It accomplishes this by "reinterpreting" the picture so that it doesn't have to record exact data for every pixel in the image. Instead, you decide how much compression you want to use. The lower the image-quality setting you use, the more compression the camera's processor uses in saving the image to memory— and the more information is irretrievably lost (and replaced with little color anomalies that seem to resemble film grain).

The first time a high-quality JPEG image is saved and then opened for viewing, it is difficult to tell that any information has been discarded at all. However, each subsequent file save recalculates the amount of data to be thrown away, and the same amount of data that was discarded in the first instance is discarded again. So the first thing you need to know about JPEG images is that when you open them, you must subsequently save them to a "lossless" format, such as TIFF (for Tagged Image File Format), or to your image editor's proprietary file format (such as Photoshop's PSD format) if you want to prevent continued image degradation.

As far as lower quality settings, the most important thing for you to remember about them is that you can never recover the image information that was lost. Each time you lower the quality setting, you raise the level of image compression—which is nothing more than further data loss. So you have to remember the same lesson you learned about reducing resolution. Once you've discarded image quality, you can never get it back, and you can almost never replace the picture you took in the first instance. Again, the only reason you should be willing to lose image quality is if your camera or computer doesn't have the capacity to store many more pictures (and you haven't had the foresight to buy extra memory cards).

Some of the more advanced digital cameras will also let you save files in either TIFF or RAW image file format. TIFF records every pixel in the exact shade of the 16 million possible colors that the image sensor could capture. Some of the best sensors can actually record a lot more than 16 million colors, thus allowing them to capture a range of brightness values closer to those found in bright, natural sunlight. That is why some cameras even let you record your images to a format called RAW (referring to untouched data as it comes directly off the sensors). RAW image files can contain as much data as your camera is designed to capture (higher cost digital cameras typically record 12 to 16 bits of information per pixel instead of the usual 8 bits per pixel). RAW image files produce extremely high-quality images, but they also create data files that are eight to sixteen times as large as those recorded for a Super High Quality (SHQ) JPEG image. You must also have (or be willing to wait for) an image editor that will allow you to process image files that contain more than 8 bits of information per pixel.

Chapter 2

Taking Care of Your Camera

B ecause a digital camera is a significant investment, it's well worth the time to learn the proper care and maintenance so your camera will continue to take good pictures over the course of its lifetime. A digital camera is a delicate piece of equipment that must be handled and maintained properly to keep it functioning correctly. This chapter covers the basic methods for caring for your camera and provides tips and pointers from an experienced user, to help you avoid learning camera care "the hard way." Just a few good habits and a bit of extra caution can save you tons of grief and make your picture-taking experience a rewarding one.

4. Keep Your Camera Handy—Safely

When you are moving about with your camera, you need to know the best ways to protect it while still allowing for convenient access. You may often need to travel over some rough terrain—from an overcrowded gathering to an overgrown path in a forest—to get the shot you want. If your camera is not protected properly, it can suffer some serious damage. Take some simple precautions, and you'll be prepared to deal with almost any situation.

Having your camera easily accessible will give you an advantage when the unexpected shots pop up. You'll want to be able to grab your camera and shoot in just a few moments, so you should have it stored in a way that allows for that. "Be prepared" should be the photographer's mantra. If you're not prepared, you just don't get the picture.

How Do I Store My Camera Properly?

Use a moisture-resistant padded case that is insulated to protect against bumps, bangs, and rapid temperature changes. Velcro-adjustable, padded partitions will keep your camera's parts and accessories from moving around as you move. You want the camera and any other breakable parts to fit snugly inside the case. If you want to carry an extra lens or other accessories, such as an external flash, find a case that provides compartments that these items fit into properly. The case should have enough room for extra batteries, memory cards, cleaning aids, and any other accessories you regularly carry. If you plan on moving about, keep your case as compact as you can, so it doesn't become cumbersome.

Keep the camera in the case when you are carrying it or storing it. If the camera is hanging around your neck it can get caught on protruding objects, take a bad knock if you slip, and swing out of control—causing damage to the camera or to you or someone close by. You want to avoid having to make the choice of protecting the camera or yourself. You can hang your camera from a belt, so you are sure you know where it is and so it won't swing around as you move.

If you are in a situation that requires you to grab shots as the moments present themselves, you should wear your camera on a neck strap. Always place the strap around your neck, or better yet, sling it over your head to the opposite shoulder like a seat belt, which is much more secure. Never, ever sling it over only your shoulder, because a practiced thief can steal it in an instant. At the least it will surely plunge disastrously to the pavement as soon as you're distracted or you take another bag off your shoulder. Digital cameras are even less forgiving than film cameras with this sort of treatment—even though you paid three or four times as much for the digital variety.

NOTE   *Better camera cases provide many compartments so you can get to needed items quickly and without rummaging. Take the time to choose a case that suits your needs and properly fits your camera and your accessories. It is a good idea to take your camera and accessories with you when you purchase a case, so you can test to see that it all fits. You don't want to leave essential pieces behind for lack of room.*

5. Keep It Dry, Cool, and Clean

Your digital camera is a delicate piece of electronic equipment and needs to be treated with respect if you are going to maintain it in good working condition. Developing good habits to start with will assure that it stays operational. One of the main threats to electronics is the environment. Severe heat and cold, rain, and dust can wreak havoc on your camera and need to be protected against.

How Do I Protect My Camera?

Common sense tells you that it's a good idea to bring an umbrella if you think it might rain. If you must, shoot only when the precipitation is fairly light and predictable, unless you have an underwater camera housing. If the wet weather is light and predictable, you'll capture the mood and atmosphere that comes with all that dampness.

When you're shooting in light precipitation, it's a good idea to invite someone along to hold the umbrella for you so your hands can be free to shoot (and to tuck the camera away if the wind shifts). If you don't have an assistant and a umbrella, look for anything that can provide temporary cover while you take the shot, such as a piece of cardboard or a newspaper—or just pull your coat over your head and camera for a makeshift hood.

Failing all that, try to find places that are covered but still provide an open view to the subject, such as a porch, large tree, or overhanging ledge. Keep your camera in its bag until you're under such protective covering. You can take nice rainy-weather shots from inside your car, either through the wet windshield or with one of the side windows opened just enough for the camera to peek past.

Severe heat and cold can cause cameras to malfunction, and in some cases damage can result. It is never a good idea to leave a camera in a car where it can be exposed to extremes of hot or cold for long periods of time. If you have to leave the camera in the car, make sure it is stored in a well-insulated case and away from direct sun (and out of sight). In extreme cold conditions, you will want to warm up the camera before switching it on. A good way to do this is to put it inside your overcoat and let your body heat do the job. If you are hiking about in cold or hot weather, it is good practice to keep the camera in its case when it is not in use.

Keeping the lens and LCD clean is the best way to keep your camera in good working order and get good, clear images. Don't use off-the-shelf cleaning solutions, your clothes, or your fingers to clean the lens or LCD. It will only make matters worse and may damage the lens. Use only supplies—tissues and a brush to wipe off dust and grime—designed for lens cleaning. You can purchase these from a camera store and you should keep them with you at all times. Actually, the best and most affordable lens-cleaning kits are those made for eyeglasses. You can buy the cloths and the lens-cleaning solution at most opticians and camera stores.

Dust and other airborne material can be hazardous to your camera. Keep the lens covered (see Tip 8, later in this chapter) and the camera in its case when dirt or debris is flying. One of the worst places you can take a camera is to the beach, especially on a windy day. Sand particles can tear up a lens or LCD in no time. If you have to shoot in such conditions, make sure you use a haze (UV) filter (see Tip 8, later in this chapter) to protect the lens, and cover the LCD with a piece of clear vinyl. Fine sand can also work its way into your camera's mechanical parts, such as the lens mount and shutter release. If this happens, it is wise to take your camera into a professional service for cleaning.

6. Make a Raincoat for Your Camera

A camera raincoat is a homemade waterproof covering for your camera that allows you to shoot in inclement weather without exposing your camera to adverse conditions.

Why Does My Camera Need a Raincoat?

Photos taken in bad weather are often dramatically striking—precisely because we don't often see such photos. Using your camera in inclement weather can be dangerous to your camera if you are not careful. If you want to capture a great shot in bad weather, though, you'll need to get out of the shelter and into the middle of things. If you are intending to shoot in wet weather, you need to take some precautions to protect your equipment. The best protection is an underwater housing, but they're not available to fit all digital cameras and they can cost as much as the camera. The next best thing is a raincoat made from a plastic bag.

How Do I Make a Raincoat for My Camera?

You will need a 2-gallon "ziplock"-type plastic bag, a haze (UV) filter, and a sunshade (always a good idea anyway because it protects your camera's lens).

1. Lay the bag flat and place the sunshade on the bag so that exactly half the shade straddles the bottom edge of the bag.

2. Trace around the sunshade with a felt-tip pen to make a half circle. Keeping the bag flat, use an Xacto knife, scissors, or a utility knife to follow the traced half circle and cut out an opening for the sunshade through both layers of the bag. After you have cut the half circle, open up the bag and you will see that it forms a full circle.

3. Now place the UV filter over the lens and screw it in. Then screw the sunshade onto the filter.

4. Place the camera inside the plastic bag and push the sunshade through the hole in the bottom.

5. Tape the plastic bag to the sunshade so that water or debris can't leak in.

These steps, and the finished raincoat, are shown in Figure 2-1.

While you're carrying the camera, keep the bag zipped shut. When you reach your location and you're ready to shoot, hold the camera so the rain won't come into the back of the bag, unzip it, and reach inside to hold the camera. Be sure to pull the bag back over your wrist. You can make a few of these raincoats ahead of time and keep them handy.

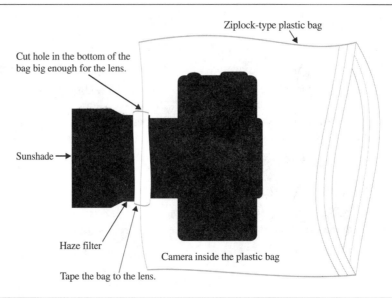

Ziplock-type plastic bag

Cut hole in the bottom of the
bag big enough for the lens.

Sunshade →

Haze filter

Tape the bag to the lens.

Camera inside the plastic bag

FIGURE 2-1 Here are the steps for making the raincoat and an example of how it should look on the camera.

NOTE *It's a good idea to slide a big, loose rubber band over the bag and around your wrist so the wind can't suddenly blow the bag over the camera, thus exposing it to the rain.*

7. Take Care of the LCD

Figure 2-2 shows an example LCD. LCDs are usually made of glass and scratch easily, so you should take care to avoid any type of impact or abrasion to that area of your camera. They are often coated with thin films to make them more viewable in glare situations, and that coating is also sensitive. You should treat the LCD as you would a pair of expensive glasses.

Why Is the LCD Important?

As emphasized in Chapter 1, the LCD is your camera's "window to the world." That wonderful little display monitor on the back of your camera provides you with a view of what your lens sees, as well as menu commands, and previews. It is an essential part of your camera, so you want to keep it in good working order. It is also one of the most vulnerable parts of your camera besides the lens.

FIGURE 2-2   The LCD is your electronic window to the world.

How Do I Protect the LCD?

Keep it clean. Use the same cleaning equipment you use on your lens. Put a piece of smooth cardboard over it with a rubber band if it doesn't have a built-in cover or protective case. Leaving a Hoodman (a cowl that you attach to the back of the camera with Velcro or an elastic strap to shade the LCD from the sun; see Chapter 15) attached can also be effective. Avoid leaving your camera in your car for extended periods of time, unless it is stored in an insulated bag or case that protects it against extreme temperatures. Glove compartments and trunks are solar ovens that can reach temperatures several times that of the outside temperature. Exposure to too much bright sunlight or extremes in temperature can also damage LCDs.

8. Keep the Lens Covered

The lens cover is a plastic or metal piece that covers and protects the lens when you are not shooting pictures. Tethers are available at camera supply stores to keep the lens cover with the camera so that it doesn't get lost in the haste of removing it from the camera. A tethered lens cap is also a good reminder to make sure the lens cover is on the lens when it is not in use. Never store the camera without making sure the lens cover is securely in place. This will keep it clean and protect it from damage. Remember, just a small impact with any hard object can permanently damage your lens.

What Kinds of Lens Covers Are Available?

Lens covers come in a few varieties:

Built-in Lens Covers   Many low-end to midrange cameras with fixed lenses come with a mechanical door that slides back to reveal the lens as soon as you turn on the camera. This is a nice feature because it automatically closes when you turn off the camera, so you'll never forget to put the lens cover back on or lose it.

Plastic Snap-on Covers   These covers are designed to fit your particular lens and have spring-loaded catches that fit into the screw threads on the inside rim of the lens. This type of lens cover tends to pop off when you unexpectedly give a fairly light nudge to one of the release handles. On the other hand, the quick-release mechanism lets you get the cover on and off quickly.

Rubber or Plastic Slip Covers   These are designed to slip snugly over the outside of the rim of your lens and must be fitted to your particular lens. These are good covers if they fit tightly enough so they don't slip off when you don't want them to.

Metal Screw-on Covers   These are the best kind of covers for absolute protection, and most professional photographers use them. They are made of tough metal and screw into the inside lens threads, making it virtually impossible for them to detach unexpectedly. Of course, your camera must have a threaded lens barrel to use a screw-on cover.

UV Filter Protection   A glass UV filter screws on the front of your lens to protect it from being scratched. After all, you can affordably replace a UV filter. If you scratch your lens, you may have to replace the entire camera. This filter has little effect if you're shooting indoors, but outdoors it has the added benefit of reducing ultraviolet haze that often softens landscape photos.

9. Keep Fresh, Quality Batteries on Hand

Cameras use either a proprietary rechargeable battery that must be purchased through the camera's manufacturer or standard AA batteries, which are readily available in many stores. You won't have much luck using standard alkaline batteries—they don't hold enough charge and thus have to be purchased more frequently (often for more than a roll of film costs).

It's a good idea to purchase a camera that uses rechargeable batteries. A number of rechargeable battery types are available, as discussed in the following sections.

Nickel Cadmium (NiCaD)   These types of batteries are the most common, but they are not necessarily the best for a couple of reasons:

- They are not environmentally friendly.

- NiCad batteries suffer from memory effect.

Memory effect is the process of a battery reducing its ability to hold a full charge when it is repeatedly recharged before it has been fully discharged. This effect increases every time the battery is recharged prematurely. It is a common problem with NiCad batteries and can render the batteries useless over time.

Nickel Metal Hydride (NiMH)   NiMH batteries are the best type of battery for use with digital cameras. They can be recharged at any time with no performance loss. They also tend to have higher power-rating capacities. They can be recharged many times before burnout. Finally, they can be recycled without damage to the environment.

Lithium Ion (LiON)   LiON batteries are mostly used in external power packs and are not readily available in AA size. They provide much more power than the other types of rechargeable batteries, so these batteries might play an important roll in future camera models.

Why Do I Need Fresh, Quality Batteries?

Keeping well-charged, high-quality batteries on hand is an important issue with digital camera use. Digital cameras draw a lot of power, because almost everything about them is electronic. You can run through batteries pretty fast if you are using a lot of the features—like the LCD, flash, and zoom lens.

It's a good idea to have at least one set of extra batteries on hand to ensure that you can make it through a normal day of shooting. You can always recharge your batteries overnight so you're good to go the next day. Of course, if you're a pro or just a fanatical hobbyist, you might want to get several sets of batteries. You can buy them at your local discount warehouse for about $20 for a set of four. Look for the power rating on the batteries. If it's not printed on the batteries, you can bet that the manufacturer isn't proud of the rating. A rating of 1600 MaH is good. Anything higher is excellent.

How Do I Tell Whether the Batteries Are Charged?

All digital cameras provide battery-life indicators on their control panels—an example is shown in Figure 2-3. The indicator is usually a symbol that looks like a battery and graphically indicates in quarter steps how much charge is left in the installed batteries.

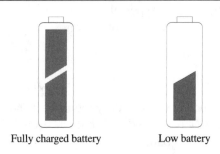

Fully charged battery   Low battery

FIGURE 2-3   The battery indicator on the control panel shows charged and low battery views.

Stay aware of the battery power level and check it at power-up and at regular intervals while you shoot, especially if you are using a lot of the electricity-hogging features like the LCD and flash. You want to be prepared so the big shot doesn't find you holding a dead camera.

How Do I Change or Recharge the Batteries?

Most digital cameras come with a battery charger, like the one shown in Figure 2-4, but this inclusion is beginning to disappear as camera prices come down. Most of the chargers that are included take a long time to recharge batteries, which is inconvenient if you use your camera a lot. Worse, if you leave the batteries in the charger for too long, they will be damaged unless the charger is smart enough to turn itself off.

Proprietary battery sizes and shapes—that is, special batteries that can be used for a single camera model only—are becoming more common. You're better off buying a camera that uses standard AA batteries, if you can. One set of proprietary batteries (an "invisible" excuse for fattening the camera manufacturer's profit margins) costs roughly twice as much as a set of four conventional AA batteries. Furthermore, if you run out or lose proprietary batteries while traveling through the Amazon, you're not going to be able to buy new ones.

It's a good idea to buy a one-hour charger and one or two extra sets of batteries. The charger device plugs into a regular wall socket and has compartments to receive the batteries. Make sure you get a charger that will receive a full set of batteries at one time. This will allow the charger to charge one set of batteries while you're using the other set. Don't leave batteries in the charger for extended periods of time beyond when they are fully charged, because they will overheat, shortening their life

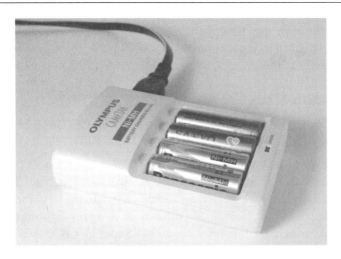

FIGURE 2-4   A typical battery charger often comes with the camera.

span. The best chargers will automatically turn themselves off as soon as the batteries are fully charged.

NiMH batteries can lose some of their charge over time, even when they are not in use, so you may need to recharge them periodically to keep them optimal. Make sure you place the batteries in the charger properly or they will not charge.

NOTE   *Remember that batteries are the lifelines for your camera, and without good power, you are dead in the water.*

10. Using and Caring for Memory Cards

Memory cards are the digital equivalent of the removable film in a conventional camera. When images are exposed on the image sensors, they are converted to electrical signals that are stored on solid-state flash memory media that take the form of small cards or disks that can be easily inserted and removed from the camera. You can keep additional cards with you to store images, should one card become full. No developing is necessary and the cards are reusable after erasing or reformatting—just like a floppy disk. They come in a range of memory capacities (which equates to the number of shots they can hold) according to the card type. The brand of camera you have will determine which type of memory card it uses.

Memory cards work with card readers, which can be attached to a computer to allow the transfer of images to other devices. Also, most current digital camera models can be attached to the computer via a USB cable so that the images can be transferred directly to the computer.

What Types and Sizes Are Available?

Various types of memory cards (see Figure 2-5) can be purchased with a variety of storage limits. The available types are explored in the following sections.

CompactFlash Types I & II   CompactFlash (CF) cards are the most popular type in use today—but only by a small margin over SmartMedia cards. CF cards are reasonably small and lightweight, fit nicely inside small digital cameras, and come protectively encased. Type I CF cards currently have an upper limit of 512MB of storage space, which is enough for about 144 Super High Quality (SHQ) 5-megapixel JPEG images.

Type II CF cards are basically the same as Type I, with the only significant difference being the thickness of the card. The Type II card is thicker to accommodate higher storage capacity or truly miniature hard drives (that actually fit right inside the card). Some CF II cards and drives will hold 1GB of memory. That's enough to get most pros through a full day of shooting without ever having to stop and download, but these cards are still rare and, as a result, they cost about $600.

FIGURE 2-5   Memory cards come in a variety of types.

SmartMedia   These are the thinnest and lightest of the memory cards. This was accomplished by taking some of the technology off the card and placing it in the camera itself. The disadvantage of the SmartMedia arrangement is that when storage capacity ability advances, the camera may not be able to use it. You can purchase cards of up to 128MB. At present, these are the second most popular memory cards—by a close margin.

One of their advantages is that, like CF cards, you can buy them almost anywhere. The other advantage of popularity is cost-per-megabyte, which is just pennies higher than the cost-per-megabyte of CF cards and significantly lower than that of the memory cards discussed in the following sections.

MemoryStick   MemoryStick is a compact memory card created by Sony and used almost exclusively in Sony products. Sony has locked its proprietary memory-card format across almost all its electronic devices, so if you buy a Sony handheld computer, you are probably more inclined to buy Sony cameras or MP3 players— just so you can use MemoryStick in all the equipment. If you don't want to be forced into making your memory choice based solely on the type of memory card used, keep the issue of exclusivity in mind.

PCMCIA PC Card   Personal Computer Memory Card International Association (PCMCIA) is a bus format invented for laptop computers. PCMCIA storage cards are only one type of device that will fit into PCMCIA slots. Digital cameras that support PCMCIA cards can also accept other types of memory media by using an adapter. PCMCIA memory cards are typically found in older, high-end, professional digital SLRs and studio-type cameras, because their large physical size allows more room for the bulkier memory card. They provide a wide range of storage capacity of up to several gigabytes.

Computer Disks   This type of camera memory is identical to the standard 3.5-inch or mini CD disks you use in the computer. The advantage is instant transferability of the camera's images to virtually any computer. The disadvantage is that the storage media will hold a limited number of pictures and is comparatively slow at both recording and transferring images. It is also impractical to store high-resolution images on floppies. Even at a relatively low JPEG quality setting, a floppy disk could barely hold one 5-megapixel image.

NOTE   *If you use more than one digital camera, it's a good idea to use the same memory type in both so you can interchange the cards.*

Why Do I Need a Memory Card?

Some low-end digital cameras can't handle memory cards. They store everything on built-in memory chips instead. This means that when the internal memory is filled, the images must be downloaded or erased before shooting can continue. Of course, that's not convenient if you're in the middle of a hike, at a wedding, or in any other situation where downloading just isn't an option.

Memory cards, on the other hand, allow you to shoot as many photos as you have cards. When you run out of space on one card, you just swap it for another.

How Do I Use Memory Cards?

Memory cards are easy to use. Check your camera's manual to make sure you get the right type.

On cameras that accept them, memory cards are installed via a small door or slot on the camera, as shown in Figure 2-6. Don't ever force the card into the slot. If you cannot easily insert it, either you have aligned it incorrectly, something is already in the slot, or the card is damaged.

FIGURE 2-6   The memory card fits into a slot in your camera.

You should never insert or remove a memory card while the camera's power is turned on, or you may damage either the data or the card. After the card is inserted properly, you can close the door and power on the camera. Some cards must be formatted the first time they are used. You will find formatting commands on your LCD menu display. After the card is formatted, it is empty and ready to take the maximum number of pictures that your camera's resolution and quality settings will allow.

Chapter 3

Understanding Shooting Modes

The advanced electronics of today's digital cameras perform automatically many of the tasks necessary for taking a photograph. The automatic or programmed mode is always a good starting point for any shot. However, as good as these automatic functions are, they are not a foolproof system. The alternative shooting modes allow for a higher degree of control, giving you options that automatic mode cannot offer in many situations. If you want to maximize your ability to capture almost any shot that comes your way, you'll need to master all the modes of your camera.

11. Understand the Shutter Release Button

The shutter release button is found on the top of the camera, typically on the right side. This button has two functions:

- Pressed halfway, it locks in the focus and exposure on the area you designate by centering it in the viewfinder.

- Fully pressed, it releases the shutter to expose the image.

If you're already familiar with photography and own a camera that automatically focuses and sets exposure, partially pressing the shutter release button is probably familiar to you. This function is exactly the same on digital cameras as it is on film cameras.

Why Do I Need to Use the Dual Modes of Operation?

Understanding the focus and exposure lock mode will let you determine exactly what part of the picture should have the sharpest focus, whether or not that object is centered in the viewfinder. Usually the object that is to be in sharpest focus is the one that needs to be best exposed, too.

How Do I Use the Shutter Release Button?

A mark, or target, in the center of your camera's viewfinder or (more often) LCD monitor indicates what object the camera is targeting to set its focus and exposure. The shape of the mark varies from camera to camera—it may be a circle, a pair of facing square brackets, or a small plus sign. (Figure 3-1 shows an example target hovering over a scene.)

You use the dual mode shutter release button in conjunction with the target to set the camera's focus and exposure. In this first exercise, I am assuming that the target of exposure and focal point are in the same place. (I will tell you how to set it up if they are not in the same place in the next exercise.) Here's how it works:

1. Place the mark in the camera's viewfinder on the spot where you want the focus to be sharpest and the exposure to be the picture's midtone. (A good midtone would equate to an average skin tone or middle to light gray. Remember that *tone* refers to the light and dark values, not the color.) When you set the exposure in this way, it will have the effect of lightening dark objects, such as shaded objects, and darkening light objects, such as a midday sky.

NOTE *To get accustomed to seeing tonal values over color values, compare color and black-and-white photographs of the same subject. You will be surprised at how some colors vary in brightness in the color photo, yet look almost identical in black and white.*

2. Without moving the camera, press the shutter release button halfway. Both focus and exposure will stay locked. Keep the shutter release button in this halfway position until you're ready to take the picture.

3. Reframe the picture so it includes the elements you want and excludes anything that's not important to the picture. (Chapter 4 offers more tips on image composition and framing a shot.)

4. Fully press the shutter release button to take the picture.

Figure 3-1 shows an example of using the target to set the shot's proper focus and exposure, and then reframing the shot for the final composition.

FIGURE 3-1   Locking the target (left) and then moving off center (right) as a way of adjusting composition

There are (rare, to be sure) times when the point of sharpest focus and the center of interest are in two different places. Here's how you work around that situation:

1. Frame your picture, placing the focus target on the object that's most important to expose correctly.

2. Press the shutter release button halfway to lock the exposure settings, and then take a look at the camera's control panel (the little LCD near the top of the camera) and make a mental note of the exposure settings shown there.

3. Change your picture-taking mode to manual and set the shutter and aperture to the same settings you saw on the control panel.

4. Now aim the target at the center of focus, press halfway to set the focus, reframe your picture so it's framed in the way that pleases you most, and press the shutter release button all the way down to take the picture. The exposure will be correct because once you've set it manually, the camera can't automatically reset the exposure.

NOTE   *Not all digital cameras feature the ability to use full manual exposure control. A few cameras, however, let you set focus and exposure separately. Since there's no hard-and-fast rule for how they all do this, you'll just have to check your camera's manual.*

Once you've taken a picture (or a series of pictures if you're in a situation where you have to shoot fast), use the LCD screen to review them. Then if you've goofed, you can immediately reshoot. It's doubly important to do this until you're pretty sure of your ability to set the camera properly, because some photo ops simply can't be re-created.

Try This: Practice Makes Perfect Timing

The difference in time between the instant the button is fully pressed and the instant you hear the "shutter sound" (or the LCD screen is temporarily blanked) is known as *shutter lag time*. If you want your digital photos to capture the very instant when a picture is taken, you need to practice anticipating the shutter lag. Practice clicking, waiting, and hearing the click until you feel you've formed the habit of shooting at just that fraction of a second before you really need to.

12. Get the Correct Color Balance

You can achieve natural-looking skin tones and other colors by using the camera's white balance controls. *White balance* is a system of balancing color components to simulate pure white under various lighting conditions so that all other colors are correctly calibrated for that condition.

Most cameras set white balance automatically as one of the options, but sooner or later, some extraneous light will "fool" the camera into setting the wrong color balance. If you preview the shot, you'll know immediately if this is the case. If so, pray that your camera lets you set white balance for a specific color of light. Daylight, indoor incandescent, indoor fluorescence, halogen lamps, and even overcast skies have unique color signatures and can be handled in cameras with white balance presets that cover these categories. Check your camera to see what presets are available. Most digital cameras that sell for over $300 will let you force a particular color balance mode.

Why Does White Balance Need to Be Set Correctly?

You need to set the white balance because different lighting sources are more intense in certain parts of the color spectrum. The type of light you're shooting in can translate to unnatural-looking colors in your photographs. For example, incandescent light gives the scene an overall yellow tint and fluorescent lights produce a blue, green, or violet cast. Light coming through clouds is bluer (cooler) than pure daylight. The light at sunset is much warmer than it is at midday. Our eyes and brain are exceptionally good at subconciously compensating for most such color casts. Your eyes rebalance the scene under given lighting conditions to look as it would look if you viewed it in daylight conditions. Technology, however, hasn't yet invented a way of printing a picture so that it rebalances the color as you view it in different lighting conditions.

The digital camera needs to know what pure white is in relation to the lighting in the scene so it can balance the colors correctly. Most of the time, this is handled automatically by the camera's electronics, but in some cases you might want to set it manually if you are still getting inappropriate color shifts in your photos.

NOTE

If you do capture color shifts in your camera, your image-editing software can do wonders in correcting them—sometimes even automatically. The only problem with this, however, is that making these corrections online takes more of your valuable time and is one more thing to learn. Otherwise, your image-editing software can probably do a better job than the camera can because it's running on a much more powerful computer than the one built into your camera.

How Do I Set White Balance?

Most of the time, the camera gets white balance right automatically under normal conditions, as long as you make sure the camera is set for automatic white balance. However, a large area of a specific man-made color or a mixture of two different types of prevailing light (like fluorescent and incandescent in the same room) can throw the camera way off.

Some cameras give you only the option of choosing the type of lighting source as a *category*—the most typical setting categories being auto, sunlight, cloudy, incandescent, and fluorescent. If the automatic mode is not working well, select one of the categories (LCD menu options) that most closely relates to the lighting condition you are in. Take a test shot to determine whether the camera corrects the color shift. You want the photo to appear as close as it can be to the way your eye sees it, and that should be your basis for comparison. You might need to experiment with the settings to get the best results for odd lighting situations. If you find you cannot get it perfect, you may be able to make some adjustments in an image-editing program.

Cameras that have more advanced manual white balance, referred to as *white preset*, are more adaptable to all lighting situations. This allows the camera to set the exact color "temperature" from reading off a white source such as a white piece of paper or a white wall. If the camera has this type of manual white balance setting, aim the camera at a white card or piece of typing paper held close to the principal subject and take a reading. This will assure 100 percent correct white balance. It's a good idea to keep a white card (or better, a Kodak 50 percent gray card) with you for this purpose since a pure white source may not always be on hand. A 50 percent gray card is a better choice because it's not as likely to be outside the range of the camera's exposure setting, and you can also use it to substitute for an incident light meter because it's neutral in both color and brightness—the perfect situation for reading with a spot meter.

13. Use Automatic and Programmed Modes

Understanding how to use the exposure modes is probably the trickiest thing you will need to learn to take great photographs. Tackle this one, and it's all downhill from there. Basically, two camera functions control the exposure of a photograph: the amount of light you let in through the lens at any given moment and the amount of time you let light come through the lens. *Aperture* controls the amount of light, and the *shutter* controls the amount of time.

What Are Automatic and Programmed Shooting Modes?

In automatic mode, the camera automatically calculates and chooses the best settings for the scene you are about to shoot; you don't need to do anything more than press the shutter release button. This is why automatic mode is often referred to as the "point-and-shoot mode."

Programmed mode is often used as a substitute for automatic mode, but it can mean more. Some cameras, such as the Nikon series, let you preprogram a number of settings, such as resolution, quality, white balance, or preset aperture or shutter (but not both), and you can save these settings to a programmed folder. That way, you can set up your own programs for situations you often encounter—such as shooting action or shooting in a backlit setting, or even for those situations best for making instant catalog photos for a commercial Web site. Other manufacturers, such as Olympus, provide a whole series of preprogrammed modes aimed at solving the problems encountered in certain typical shooting situations. Commonly found preset mode settings include night scenes, snow scenes, backlit scenes, and action (sports) scenes. Then, if you're going to shoot in one of those situations, you just set the camera's mode dial or make a choice on the LCD menu. As long as you're shooting fast-action sports and your camera is in action mode, you're likely to get a high percentage of well-exposed photos without having to give it any further thought at all. Ideally, it's nice to have a choice between both methods of mode setting. Custom mode setting (exemplified by the Nikon approach mentioned previously) is terrific for special situations that are unique to your personal needs.

Why Do I Need to Use Automatic Mode?

Using modes cuts the time it takes for you to set and balance your camera's settings when shooting in situations that are common but that require a different set of exposure settings than the "ideal" or "normal" situation (bright sunlight coming from behind your shoulder, is considered "normal" by camera manufacturers). Instead of having to study what to do, you just turn the dial or click the menu button to choose the situation you're in. That gives you the best chance of getting a good shot quickly (for shots like the one shown in Figure 3-2).

Eventually, you should learn how to adjust your camera's settings yourself, because exceptions to the camera's preset modes do occur and because settings for one type of situation can be perfect for other situations. Automatic mode is not a cure-all, so it's good for you to understand the shutter and aperture *priority* modes (see Tips 15 and 16 later in this chapter) that can offer more optimal results when you have the time to use them. *Shutter-priority mode* lets you choose a specific

FIGURE 3-2   Photographing an animal is the kind of spontaneous shot that leaves you with no time for complex setup.

shutter speed while the camera chooses the correct aperture for proper exposure. *Aperture-priority mode* lets you choose the exact aperture you want while the camera chooses the shutter speed. You use shutter-priority mode when you know you want to freeze motion or intentionally blur it. You use aperture-priority mode when *depth-of-field* (the distance over which everything is in sharp focus) is the most important consideration. In sports photography, shutter priority is virtually indispensable. In portraiture, aperture priority is needed because you want to force the background to blur by using the widest available aperture (f-stop).

How Do I Use the Camera in Automatic (Point-and-Shoot) Mode?

Some cameras allow you to use automatic mode by selecting a position on the mode switch, and others require that you select the mode from the LCD menu. Most cameras will default to automatic mode unless you specifically set the camera to not do so. The camera uses its sensors to make its best guess at the proper *f-stop* (denoted as f-2.8, f-3.5, and so on) and shutter speed required for a good exposure. All you have to do is point and shoot.

NOTE   *Always return your camera to automatic mode before you move on to the next shooting location. You'll then have the best chance of getting at least an acceptable picture when there's no time to prepare.*

14. Use Manual Mode

In manual mode, the aperture and exposure controls are set entirely by the photographer. The camera can't change these settings on its own. If you want to set focus manually, that's usually a separate operation and the ability to do that is even rarer than the ability to set exposure in full manual mode. The purpose of manual mode is to give you complete control over exposure.

Why Do I Need Manual Mode?

Manual mode is most appropriate for situations in which you want to use a particular aperture or shutter speed and also want to overexpose or underexpose the image deliberately. An example for using manual mode would be shooting a high-key glamour portrait. You want to use the camera's maximum aperture to keep depth-of-field as shallow as possible. At the same time, the shot should be "overexposed" by one or two stops so that skin tones are lighter and more delicate than usual and the eyes are brighter, more piercing, and more sensitive looking than usual. Another instance in which full manual mode is required is the situation in which it is impossible for the camera to calculate the proper exposure automatically, such as in the fireworks photo shown in Figure 3-3. Most of the area in the photo is of the night sky, but the point of interest is the bright light from the fireworks, which would have hardly registered on the camera's built-in meter. Also, a long exposure was required to give the fireworks time to create a light trail.

Using manual mode is also a good way to teach yourself how to master the camera. You can easily experiment with what happens when you vary the combination of aperture and shutter speed. Best of all, most digital cameras place extensive image information (called EXIF data) in the header of each

FIGURE 3-3   This is an example of a subject that is best shot in manual mode.

JPEG file—so it's easy to use your camera's image transfer software, an image-cataloging program, or the browser in either of the current versions of Photoshop (7 and Elements 2.0) to show you the image, while providing the specifications on how that image was shot. In other words, you can compare what it took to blur the flying hair in one shot to what it took in another that is perfectly exposed but features razor-sharp strands of flying hair and a background that is out of focus. Taking the time to learn manual mode operation can spell the difference between a snapshot and a great photograph, and it gives you the power to tackle any situation.

How Do I Use the Camera in Manual Mode?

1. Take a meter reading for the overall brightness of your subject by shooting a test shot in automatic mode.

2. Preview the test shot on your LCD monitor. Most cameras will show the exposure that was used superimposed on the image.

3. Use the mode switch on your camera to put the camera in manual mode. Some cameras allow you to do this with a simple position on the mode switch and others require that you select it from the LCD menu.

4. After you set up manual mode, use the jog control and/or the mode dial to adjust the shutter speed and f-stop to the desired levels. You'll have to check your camera's manual to see how your particular model works.

5. Check your camera's control panel. If your camera was well designed, you will be able to preview the effect of the manual settings in the LCD. If not, simply shoot a test shot and then review it to see how close your settings come to the effect you want.

The following list provides manual setting guidelines that work for a range of typical situations. These guidelines will give you a good starting point. You can then fine-tune the settings to meet specific requirements.

- **To stop motion**   Set the camera to the highest shutter speed that will give you a correct exposure at or near the widest possible aperture (smallest f-stop number).

- **To blur motion**   Set your camera at a fairly slow shutter speed, but not too much slower than 1/60.

- **To blur the foreground and background**   Use the widest aperture and then raise your shutter speed to compensate.

- **To maximize the overall sharpness of the image from as close to the camera as possible to as far from the camera as possible**   Use the smallest f-stop (largest number) to narrow the aperture as much as possible. Most digital cameras will not step down their apertures to an opening smaller than f-11.

You can keep the exposure level constant by reducing the f-stop by one setting each time you increase the shutter speed by one setting—and vice versa. This counterbalancing of aperture and shutter speed settings allows you to choose between controlling depth-of-field (aperture) or stop action or blurred motion (shutter speed) while maintaining a balanced exposure.

The following table shows settings that cameras typically use for shutter speed (top row) and f-stop settings (bottom row). The settings are often slightly more or less than a full setting (called an *exposure value* or EV) because of the mechanics traditionally used in the manufacture of 35mm cameras.

Shutter speed (in seconds)	1/4	1/8	1/15	1/30	1/60	1/125	1/250	1/500	1/1000
f-stop (aperture)	f-1.5	f-2.0	f-2.8	f-3.5	f-5.6	f-8	f-11	f-16	f-22

A nice thing about digital cameras is that they let you see the effects of changing the setup in your LCD preview. The LCD preview will show the changes in exposure so you can easily see the optimal settings in advance. Using film is much trickier and requires a lot of experience to get it right (plus, it's not immediate). If the subject doesn't move or can be posed, even expert film photographers will take a range of exposures (called *bracketing*) to make sure they get the shot that's most favorable to the subject. Remember, however, that sometimes the "wrong" exposure is the happiest of accidents. Digital cameras eliminate a lot of the guesswork, but you can still take all the credit for the "perfect" exposure.

15. Set Aperture Priority

The aperture controls the amount of light that comes through the lens at any given instant. Within the lens of the camera is a diaphragm called an *iris* that opens and closes according to automatic or manual settings. It is named after (and is much like) the iris in your eye. The size of the iris's opening is referred to as the *aperture*. Changing the aperture settings adjusts the size of the opening and thus the amount of light the lens passes through to the image sensor.

What Is Aperture-Priority Mode?

When you lock in the aperture setting as a priority, the camera is forced to adjust the shutter speed relative to the aperture setting. This is called *aperture-priority mode*. This is different than fully automatic mode, in which the camera determines both the aperture and shutter speed for you.

Why Do I Need to Use Aperture-Priority Mode?

Aperture priority is used when you want to be able to control depth-of-field or ensure either the fastest (by opening the aperture as far as possible) or the slowest (by closing the aperture as much as possible) shutter speed. Higher f-stop numbers indicate a smaller aperture, smaller f-stop numbers indicate a larger aperture. Go figure, but that's just the way it is.

Control Depth-of-Field   Depth-of-field is the distance between the closest sharply focused object to the lens and the farthest sharply focused object from the lens. Smaller apertures (higher f-stop numbers) create greater depth-of-field. Wide apertures create very shallow depth-of-field.

The other factor that influences depth-of-field is the focal length of the lens. The focal length of digital camera lenses, as stated on the lens barrel, is misleading because it is almost always stated as the equivalent of the focal length of a 35mm camera. This relation works as far as the equivalent angle of view is concerned. However, it is the actual distance of the camera lens to the film plane that determines depth-of-field. The shorter the focal length, the greater the depth-of-field. The size of the image sensor in most digital cameras is between one-half and one-quarter that of a 35mm film frame. As a result, the lens must be one-half to one-quarter the distance from the film plane in order to get the same angle of view. At the same time, you get two to four times the depth-of-field. If you have a camera that gets less than 3 megapixels of resolution and your lens is zoomed to about 50mm (normal field of view) equivalency, focusing on an object 10 feet away will put everything in focus from about 3 feet to infinity. If you are shooting close-ups or portraits and want to blur the background at all, you must shoot at the widest possible aperture. It's also a good idea to zoom out as far as possible.

The latest generation of very high resolution digital cameras have image sensors that are about two-thirds the size of a 35mm film frame. These cameras will give you quite a bit more aperture control over depth-of-field because their lens focal lengths have to be longer in order to accommodate the larger physical image size.

NOTE   *You also can change apparent depth-of-field after you've shot the picture by using your image-editing program's selection tools and blurring filters (see Tip 64 in Chapter 9).*

Learning to control depth-of-field gives you one method of isolating the subject from its background. Sometimes, for example, you want to blur the background and focus in on the nearer subject (as shown in Figure 3-4). At other times, you want everything you are viewing to be in clear focus. The aperture setting will give you at least some control over depth-of-field.

Ensure the Fastest or the Slowest Shutter Speed   Because the aperture can limit the amount of light that gets in through the lens, you must adjust the camera's exposure times to compensate. Opening the aperture wide will allow for the fastest possible shutter speed in any given lighting condition. Faster shutter speeds will accommodate stop-action photography or provide a steady shot when conditions make it impossible to hold the camera still.

NOTE   *Remember that the aperture settings are inverse to the size of the aperture. Larger f-stops produce smaller openings for light.*

FIGURE 3-4   Changing depth-of-field can be used to blur unwanted detail in the background.

How Do I Use Aperture-Priority Mode?

1. Set the camera to aperture-priority mode by using the mode control or selecting aperture-priority mode from the LCD preview menu.

2. Use the appropriate knob, jog control, or menu selection to change the aperture setting or f-stop up or down, depending on your focus and shutter speed requirements.

NOTE   *Another way to affect the speed of exposure is to change the camera's ISO (International Standards Organization) rating. Digital ISO numbers are designed to be equivalent to film ISO speed ratings (for example, ASA 100, 200, and so on). This is a way of changing the image sensors' sensitivity to light. In the digital world, higher ISO settings increase the voltage noise and pictures appear grainier. So when the need for fast shutter speed is not an issue, a lower ISO is better. That is why most digital cameras default to their lowest ISO settings. On the other hand, faster film is also grainier—so the viewing audience is used to seeing this condition when candids are shot in dim lighting conditions. You can change the ISO settings through the LCD menu.*

16. Set Shutter Priority

You can manually set the shutter speed to have the camera calculate the appropriate aperture setting.

Why Do I Need to Use Shutter Priority?

Shutter priority will allow you to control how you photograph objects in motion. Shutter priority is the mode to use when you want to increase or reduce the amount of blurring in the picture that's due to the movement of either the subject or the camera. You can achieve some interesting special effects by slowing the shutter speeds to blur moving objects (such as water in a waterfall) while the surroundings remain in sharp focus. This adds a suggestion of motion that can be very dramatic. By using shutter priority with higher speed settings, you can freeze moving objects, as is often the case in sports photography. Not setting the shutter speed high enough can result in blurred shots, as Figure 3-5 shows.

FIGURE 3-5   Shooting photos while you are dancing is not advised unless you have the shutter speed maxed.

How Do I Use Shutter-Priority Mode?

1. Set the camera to shutter priority by moving the mode control to the appropriate position, or choose priority mode from an LCD menu.

2. Use the appropriate knob, jog control, or menu selection to change the speed settings, which are designated in fractions of seconds or in full seconds (which is usually reserved for evening or nighttime photography).

3. If, for example, the display shows 1/250, this means it is set at one two-hundred-and-fiftieth of a second, which is a safe speed for most handheld shooting. Set the camera at the highest possible shutter speed that's consistent with the brightness of the prevailing light. Make a test shot to see what that is.

Many cameras can go up to 1/1500 and higher, which can stop a race car in its tracks. A setting of 1/4 is good for blurring swift-moving water, but you will have to shoot with your camera on a tripod in order to keep the surrounding landscape sharp. If you go beyond a setting that the camera can adjust for with the aperture, you will most likely see a flashing red light close enough to the viewfinder that your eye pressed against it can see it. The flashing red light is warning you that the picture you are about to take is either overexposed or underexposed. Warnings are a help, but you need to learn to trust your own judgment more than the camera's.

17. Use Macro Mode for a Closer Look

Macro focusing refers to a camera's ability to focus at very close distances (3 feet or less) and magnify a small part of an object or scene so that it fills the entire image sensor, much like a magnified image fills the view while you're using a low-power microscope.

Digital cameras vary in their ability to take macro shots, so if you like close-up photography, the closest possible distance at which the subject can be in focus is something to consider when choosing a camera. Most digital cameras can focus to distances closer than are typical with film cameras, because a digital camera's sensors are typically one-third to two-thirds (for cameras starting at 4-megapixel resolution) the size of a 35mm frame. As a result of the small sensor size, the lens must be much closer to the sensor to provide a "normal" field of view. The closer the lens is to the sensor, the greater the depth-of-field. Most digital cameras, regardless of price, focus down to between 2 and 4 feet. However, some digital cameras, such as those in the Nikon Coolpix series, can shoot at distances well under 1 inch from the lens, which can make a fly look like a prehistoric monster. Figure 3-6 shows a close-up shot.

Why Do I Need Macro?

There is an old saying in photography: "If you think you are too close, get closer." The macro is your chance to get even closer. The most common error made by amateur photographers is failure to move in on their subjects to fill the frame with only the details they need for the shot. Close-up shooting is a good way to break this habit and discover a wonderful world of details that most of us overlook (or can't see). Macro mode is extremely valuable if you like studying the abstractions inherent in close-ups and is often helpful for recording small details used in scientific research, police evidence, or printed documents.

FIGURE 3-6   This macro shot gives you the bee's eye view.

How Do I Use Macro Mode?

1. Read your camera's specifications to determine what macro ranges it can handle.

2. Turn on macro mode. Some cameras force you to enter macro mode from the camera's LCD menu. Most cameras come with a macro button. Toggling the macro button to its on position increases the distance of the lens from the sensor, which lets the camera achieve closer than normal focusing.

3. You can usually tell when macro mode is turned on by looking for a flower icon on the camera's control panel LCD.

4. Turn on your camera's LCD and move in on your subject as close as necessary. Then partially press the shutter release button. If the camera won't focus, either you're outside macro focusing range or you've turned off autofocus.

5. Once the image is focused, you may discover you'd like to change the framing. You may be able to move in even closer and get sharp focus. If not, back off a bit.

NOTE

When using macro mode, it's a good idea to work in aperture-priority mode so that you can use a small aperture to increase depth-of-field. Remember that lower aperture means slower shutter speeds, so you might need to use a tripod. This is especially important because at close distances, small camera movements can dramatically change your framing.

If you're shooting outdoors, use something as a windbreak, because any movement in close-up shots is hard to deal with, as everything, including movement, is amplified. A piece of cardboard, such as the sun protector in your vehicle, can work well as a windbreak. In a pinch, use your own body as a windbreak by putting your back to the wind while shooting. Check your focus in the LCD and take test shots.

18. Use Burst Mode to Capture the Moment

Burst mode (also called rapid sequence or continuous) allows the camera to record a rapid sequence of still shots (usually at the rate of two to five shots per second) by storing them directly to the camera's internal memory and not onto the memory card. The amount and the speed at which this can happen is determined by

- The size of your camera's memory

- The speed of data transfer

- Your currently chosen resolution

Obviously, smaller images use less data space, so they can be recorded much faster. You will need to check your camera's specifications to determine its specific burst mode capabilities.

Figure 3-7 shows a series of shots taken of a subject in motion in burst mode.

Why Do I Want to Create a Rapid Sequence?

One of the best reasons for shooting in rapid sequence is to help you capture the peak moment in an action shot. Remember the shutter lag time mentioned in Tip 11 earlier in this chapter? The workaround is to put your camera in burst mode and start shooting about half a second before the peak of the action will occur

FIGURE 3-7   This series of shots was taken of a skateboarder as she moved across the parking lot. I followed her motion with the camera in burst mode.

(think of the moment the bat hits the ball). By shooting at 1/3 second intervals, you're more likely to catch that peak.

Burst mode also avoids another significant lag time associated with normal shooting modes—the time between shots as the camera offloads the images to the memory card. Burst mode bypasses that action and postpones storing the images to the card or disk until the whole sequence is finished. In Las Vegas terms, when you use burst mode, you are hedging your bet.

Before you get too excited about burst mode, check your camera's specifications to determine whether burst mode is available. Also, the more images you can shoot with one burst and the shorter the interval between individual frames, the better your chances of capturing that peak moment. (See Chapters 7 and 13 for more information on shooting in burst mode.)

How Do I Use Burst Mode to Shoot a Rapid Sequence?

1. Choose the resolution at which you want to shoot in burst mode. If you want the best resolution for the frame you finally select, it's worth considering a compromise at the second highest quality setting for JPEG compression. Keep your image resolution at the maximum your camera can shoot. If capturing the peak moment is more important than getting the best quality, lower both the quality and resolution by as much as you think you can tolerate.

2. To shoot, you need to get the camera in a stable position, so a tripod is a good idea. Any movement in the camera will make the sequence jumpy if you later want to use it in an animation. Half press the shutter release button to lock in focus and exposure. When you are ready to shoot the sequence, press the shutter release all the way down and hold it until the burst is complete.

3. At the end of the burst, the warning light near your viewfinder will start flashing as the camera offloads the sequence to your memory card. When the flashing stops, you can jog through the images in preview mode. If you don't like what you see, erase those images and try again.

19. Use Time-Lapse Mode

Most of us have seen time-lapse photography in all those wonderful nature films that show a flower opening up or a butterfly emerging from a cocoon. These are motion sequences shot over a long period of time and then shown in rapid succession to give the illusion that the transformation is happening in real time. Time-lapse mode is the opposite of burst mode. Time-lapse compresses slow motion into a smaller window of time, whereas burst mode captures microseconds of very fast motion as a series of stills.

Why Should I Use Time-Lapse Mode?

Time-lapse photography can give you a clearer look at things that move slowly when contrasted with the hyperactivity that usually surrounds us. If you want to demonstrate how something changes over an extended period of time, this is a mode you'll appreciate. Figure 3-8 shows an example.

NOTE   *You don't need a time-lapse mode on your camera to capture action over extended periods of time. Richard Misrach, a photographer in Berkeley, California, made an astonishing series of photographs by shooting a picture once a week of the view from his second-story deck in the hills overlooking San Francisco Bay (*Richard Misrach: Golden Gate. *Arena Editions, 2001).*

How Do I Use Time-Lapse Mode to Create a Sequence of Shots Over Time?

Many cameras have built-in technology that helps greatly with producing time-lapse sequences. The computer in the camera is used to set a fixed time interval between shots. The feature is similar to the self-timer, except it keeps repeating shots. The camera will shoot automatically according to how you set it or until it runs out of storage or batteries. Once again, you will need to use a tripod to steady the camera while the sequence is being shot.

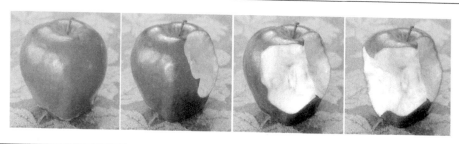

FIGURE 3-8   Time-lapse photography closely connects events that happen over an extended period of time.

Because the time interval for the total sequence can be extensive, you need to pay attention to the environmental conditions. The lighting, weather, or position of the subject may change over time. You will need to take that into consideration and apply the controls as needed to maintain a consistent environment over the length of the shoot—which can be minutes, hours, days, or longer. You may need special lighting or protection from wind, for example. How you handle this depends on how ambitious you are. Most of all, you will need patience. Time-lapse photography is challenging, but it's also rewarding, and the photographs you take will certainly get compliments.

NOTE   *Many digital cameras ship with, or can be used with, an AC adapter. If your time-lapse sequence will take place over more than 24 hours, you'd best plug in your camera with an AC adapter so that you don't run out of battery power. If you're out in the wilderness, you can use an external battery pack. These typically sell for around $50 and last about four times longer than the camera's internal batteries.*

20. Use Video and Audio Modes

In these modes, the camera acts as a video camera or voice recorder for short periods of time. Some cameras have only video capabilities. For audio, the camera must be equipped with a microphone. The video and audio are typically about half the quality of movies shot on an old-fashioned, low-tech camcorder. However, it is rare that you can shoot sequences that last more than a minute. The best use for these "video-ettes" is for Web or e-mail animation, or you can insert them into presentation programs, such as Microsoft PowerPoint.

Shooting digital video is much like shooting in burst mode, except video mode uses much lower resolution images so that it can shoot at a much higher frame rate than burst mode. Standard video will shoot at 30 frames per second to be able to fool the eye into seeing a continuous motion without any perception of individual frames. Digital still-camera videos, on the other hand, typically record at 10 to 15 frames per second. However, at the small maximum size in which they're usually filmed, the motion in digital format seems reasonably smooth and natural.

Most cameras record to one or more of the following file formats: MPEG (Motion Picture Experts Group), AVI (the Windows movie standard), or MOV (QuickTime). (See Chapter 7 for more on moving pictures.) All these formats have a strong following and support, but QuickTime files are definitely the most Web and cross-platform friendly. These file formats have built-in compression algorithms that reduce the amount of information needed to be stored for each frame. Much of the resulting loss of quality is hidden by the fact that the viewer sees each frame for too short a time to register small defects on the mind's eye.

Why Do I Need to Record Video or Audio?

The low quality of digital videos shot by most digital cameras is actually perfectly appropriate for motion sequences that are to be used as attention-catchers on Web sites or PowerPoint presentations. That is because the lower quality results in smaller files that can load and play faster over Internet connections, and that take up a smaller part of the Web page display. These same qualities make still-camera videos ideal for e-mailing a baby's first steps or the first kiss of newlyweds.

Also, digital cameras have the convenient feature of writing the video directly into digital video format, saving them as QuickTime or MPEG files. It is much easier to place these preformatted files into a presentation or onto a Web page. Let's face it, if you're shooting video with a digital camera, you are probably not trying to make an edited film. You simply want some simple motion that calls attention to whatever is being presented or that demonstrates a process that's difficult and boring to explain in words. If the camera records audio, you can even say a personal hello to your Web site's visitors.

How Do I Set Up and Record Video and Audio?

1. It is best to use the highest-capacity memory card you can afford so that you have room to shoot scenes more than once. Movies devour card storage space.

2. Place the camera in video mode via the control mode selector or the LCD.

3. Half press the shutter release button to lock in the autofocus and exposure. Then fully press the shutter and hold it down to start recording.

4. The display will let you know how much time you have left to record with a countdown meter.

5. You can stop the recording at any time by letting up on the shutter release button.

6. As soon as you end the recording, the camera will begin offloading the video frames to your memory card. This may take a few seconds, so don't turn off the camera while the transfer to the memory card is taking place.

21. Photograph Documents and Artwork

Documents and artwork are flat, two-dimensional material that is textual or graphical in nature. This could be documents like letters, signs, and books, or graphics pieces like drawings, paintings, and illustrations.

Why Does Shooting Documents and Artwork Need Special Consideration?

If the piece you want to shoot is not set up properly—in terms of orientation to the camera and lighting—your shot will suffer from *keystone distortion,* in which the edge farthest from the camera appears smaller than the closer opposite edge; poor focus; color distortion; and almost certainly lighting glare on the surface of the document.

How Do I Set Up and Shoot Documents and Artwork?

1. Be sure your camera has a macro mode if you are shooting pieces that are closer to the camera than its normal focusing distance permits. This will usually be the case if you are copying small documents such as postage stamps or business cards.

2. If your camera's macro mode doesn't allow you to focus close enough, check the Web site of a major online camera store (such as http://www.bhphoto.com) for supplementary macro lenses that are compatible with your camera. These are usually quite reasonable in cost.

3. Mount the camera on a tripod and make sure the camera is parallel to the document in the vertical and horizontal directions. It is a common mistake to lean a work against the wall and not realize that the angle of the lean will cause keystone distortion if you do not tilt the camera at the same angle.

4. If possible, set the color balance manually. If that is not possible, set the preset closest to the lighting you are using.

5. For shooting documents, use a high-contrast document mode or (second best) a black-and-white mode if one is available on your camera. Light

evenly from both sides of the document. The lights should be matched lights at 45-degree angles to the document surface and at equal distances from the center of the piece. The light distribution should be even across the document. If you are shooting small art, another good solution is to buy an inexpensive copy stand from a professional photography store. This will allow you to lay the document flat and also provides brackets for mounting your camera lights.

6. A polarizing filter may help to kill reflections. Don't use glass over your artwork unless you are willing to polarize all your lights and your camera lens, which can be quite a project and quite an expense for an inexperienced shooter.

Figure 3-9 shows the copy stand setup for photographing documents.

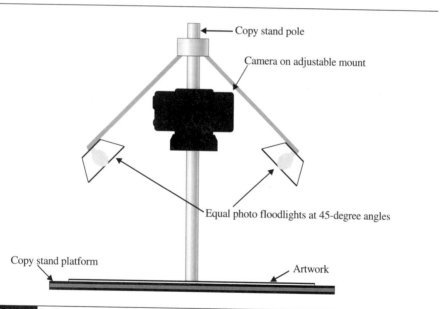

Copy stand pole

Camera on adjustable mount

Equal photo floodlights at 45-degree angles

Copy stand platform

Artwork

FIGURE 3-9   Copy stand method for document shooting

Chapter 4

Composing, Focusing, and Metering

This chapter shows you some of the optimal procedures for ensuring that you get the best pictures out of whatever photo opportunity happens to present itself. Remember, the prime photo ops often come when you least expect them. So if you know the basic rules for composing your photo, if you focus on what you want to be the center of attention, and if you use proper metering to make sure your picture isn't too light or too dark—you'll have done most of what you need to do to ensure a winner. The only remaining trick is learning to capture exactly the right 1/100 of a second.

22. Understand How Good Composition Holds Viewer Interest

Composition refers to how the elements of an image fit together. Finding a good subject to photograph is not enough in itself. Shooting it in a way that is original, cohesive, attractive, and powerful is what will make the photograph memorable. The process is called *image composition*, but is generally referred to simply as composition.

In Figure 4-1, you can see that the photograph of the waterfall on the left is cut off on every side so your eye keeps moving to the edges in an attempt to see what was not included. The image seems incomplete, which produces a tension within the viewer. On the right is a well-composed photo of the same waterfall. There is a clear foreground, middle ground, and background. The water can be seen in its entirety, and the view is contained by the cliffs which draw your eye to the waterfall as the center. This photograph allows the viewer to relax and focus on the cascading water.

FIGURE 4-1   By looking at these two shots of the same subject, you can see the photo on the right is a more dynamic composition.

Why Do I Need Good Composition?

Achieving good composition is not a trivial accomplishment and is extremely important in producing an excellent photograph. Good composition focuses the viewer's attention and interest and provides a visually dynamic experience.

The best compositions work on multiple levels, so that color, light, shapes, and subject matter all work together as a whole. We've all spent hours looking at the usual family snapshots, and we understand the difference between a good photograph and a lackluster one. Subject matter, body language, facial expression, the backdrop or setting, and the play of light are all important contributors to the greatness of a photograph—but in most cases, the deciding difference is composition.

How Do I Achieve Good Composition?

You need to consider a number of factors when setting up a composition: the selection and arrangement of the elements, the framing of the elements, the shot's focal point, and the symmetry of the photo.

Artists use the Rule-of-Thirds to produce dynamic compositions. The rule is based on the ancient Greek concept of the "golden rectangle"—basically the same shape as a normal photograph. To use the rule, draw two imaginary vertical and two imaginary horizontal lines in the rectangle of the frame to divide it into thirds, both horizontally and vertically. By placing the elements in the composition on each of the grid intersections, a pleasing and balanced arrangement results. Figure 4-2 shows a good example of the Rule-of-Thirds in a photograph. After a while, you'll develop an intuitive sense for this kind of balance if you are aware as you practice.

Selecting the Essential Elements   The essential elements of a shot are the objects or settings that relate to your subject. Try to pare down your subject matter to the bare essentials. Everything in a photograph should be included for a reason, not just because it was there. Although you can remove or alter certain details later with image-editing software, you need to understand what you are shooting and try to frame it in a way that captures the most concise image to express that understanding. If there are elements in the background or foreground that you want to be sure to include or exclude, adjust your depth-of-field to bring them in or out of focus. Change the orientation of the camera to vertical if that frames the scene better. Get close in and fill the frame with the subject or parts of the subject. The best way to capture the essentials in a photo is to experiment—move around and explore your options. Take a number of photos using different compositions, because there is never just *one* solution. Remember, taking extra digital photos costs you absolutely nothing and it is the best and quickest route to learning to

FIGURE 4-2   Notice how the photo is composed so that the important elements align with the thirds of the grid.

be a good photographer. The best photographers are those who know what to throw away.

Arranging the Key Elements   The key elements of the composition need to be arranged in relation to the whole frame and to each other. This includes the relationship of objects, background, light, and color. The arrangements in a shot can be considered on both a two-dimensional plane (strictly as flat shapes on paper) or in three-dimensions (foreground, middle, background, and perspective). The orientation of the camera can play a factor here, too. Study the composition of professional photographs and see how they balance all of these elements in unconventional ways.

Most of us, when starting out, tend to place the focal point at the center of the frame and not give too much consideration to other elements surrounding it. Try to give every element of a photo an equal level of importance, and a major door of perception will open for you. Don't be afraid to try unique approaches to taking your photos that might involve shooting from odd angles, adjusting the lighting, shooting at different times of day, or getting very close to the subject—to name a few. Swiveling LCD viewfinders give digital photographers unique opportunities for unusual viewpoints.

Framing the Photo   The frame represents the extent of the image that will be captured by the camera's image sensors. What you see when you look through the viewfinder will tell you the extent of the frame in most cases.

Optical viewfinders can suffer from parallax problems at close shooting distances, which can skew the frame boundaries up, down, or sideways. (See Tip 24 later in the chapter for more information on parallax problems.) Some cameras give you an indication of the shift to help you compensate, but some don't do this, so you need to learn how to accommodate parallax problems through experience. For close-ups, you may find it more accurate to use the LCD to frame your shots.

Pay careful attention to any subject matter that is intersected by the frame boundary. The human eye tends to suppress detail at the periphery of vision, so it is common for new photographers not to notice the frame edges when shooting a photograph, only to be surprised later when they see how much detail was lurking in those portions of the picture. Be aware that the camera registers more than you do, so you need to look at all parts of the frame carefully to set up composition correctly.

Finding the Focal Point of the Picture   The focal point is the main point of interest in the photo composition. This is *not* necessarily the center of the frame. (See the information on the Rule-of-Thirds in the section "How Do I Achieve Good Composition?" earlier in this chapter.)

Two things—clear focus and position—define the focal point. The eye will move to the sharpest detail in the photograph first. Then the eye will move through the image guided by placement, color, contrast, perspective, and visual connections. You want the viewer's eye to stay within the composition at all times, so be careful of elements that carry the eye out of the frame. Try using the focus lock to move the focal point off center and balance that with other elements on the opposite side. This creates a more dynamic and exciting image. Few things in life are perfectly symmetrical on a one-for-one basis—not even the human face. So if you center objects, the composition usually feels unnatural. While that might be okay if you intended it and it helps the shot, centering the main point of interest often tends to make the image static—unmoving and boring.

Figure 4-3 shows how elements of perspective can draw the viewer to a focal point of the bird, then up and out into the sky. The movement of your eye mimics the motion of the roller coaster, giving the viewer a visceral connection with the subject.

FIGURE 4-3   All the visual elements should work to support the focal point of the photograph. In this image, the perspective draws you into the composition.

Using Symmetry in the Arrangement   Symmetry comes in two basic forms: *static* symmetry is balanced around a central axis, and *dynamic* symmetry uses proportional arrangement to create a less obvious solution. Both produce a stable, balanced image, but static symmetry has a more graphical feel. Dynamic symmetry has greater flexibility and a more natural look.

Again, you should try to overcome the tendency to place the focal point of the photo dead center in the frame. Lock on your target and then try moving the camera off the focal point to develop a dynamic symmetry with the subject matter.

23. Understand Focus

Focus is the ability of the camera lens to bring to clarity the most important part(s) of an image's detail (see Chapter 3).

What Are the Types of Focusing Systems?

Most cameras offer three types of focusing systems:

■ **Autofocus**   A system for adjusting focus automatically by means of a sensor on the front of the camera and a motor for moving the lens in the camera in and out. This is a hands-free solution to focusing and it works amazingly well most of the time.

■ **Manual focus**   Focus is achieved manually by you either turning the lens (on cameras that provide this), adjusting a menu distance slider, or selecting a fixed distance.

■ **Fixed focus**   Allows for focus at one preset distance. It is limited to low-end cameras, such as those throwaway point-and-shoots that get left at the processing lab. Lately, some low-resolution, under-$50 point-and-shoot digital cameras have begun to appear that have fixed-focus lenses.

Why Do I Need to Pay Attention to Focus?

Since focal points in a photo are most commonly delineated by sharp focus, it is paramount to control which areas of the picture are in focus and which ones are not if you care about the quality of your photos. The human eye is constantly scanning and readjusting focus, which produces the impression that everything is in focus all the time. In actuality, however, we focus only on a small part of our visual field at any instant. This dictates how we view photographs, because a human viewer will naturally fix on the sharpest detail immediately. The camera does not have that luxury, so you will need to understand and control what the camera is focusing on. Sometimes, intentionally blurring objects in a shot can be a nice effect, especially in foregrounds and backgrounds or to create a motion effect.

Figure 4-4 shows examples of how focus can affect an image. Clockwise, the motorcycle riders are blurred in a way that indicates motion, the leaf shows the sharp detail of a close macro shot, the sharper focus in the center draws you to the eye and holds you there, and finally the use of background blurring accentuates the larger flower.

FIGURE 4-4   Examples of how focus can affect an image

How Do I Focus the Camera Properly?

You focus the camera in three basic ways: via autofocus, manual focus, and fixed focus. Autofocus and manual focus are most pertinent to digital photographers. Only the very cheapest of digital cameras have fixed focus. These cameras have such extreme depth-of-field that it is almost impossible to get anything out of focus.

Autofocus is achieved in one of two ways:

- **Continuous autofocus**   Doesn't lock when you lock the exposure, and the camera follows focus, regardless of how rapidly the subject moves and changes position. Continuous autofocus is absolutely necessary when shooting fast-moving subjects. Otherwise, they won't be in the same position when the shutter is fired as they were in when you first pressed the shutter button to focus. Continuous autofocus is also used for making movies and shooting sporting events.

- **Locked autofocus**   The focus remains set at the focusing distance set by the camera when you put the camera in lock mode by partially pressing the shutter release button.

Try This: Getting Around Tricky Autofocus Situations

If you are shooting through some close-up object, such as branches, a fence, or blinds, the autofocus sensors will be confused. Bright or fast-moving objects can also confuse autofocus sensors. If you find that your camera is arbitrarily changing focus, try to find a nearby object that is the same distance from the camera as the object you want to focus on; then half press the shutter release button to lock the focus, keep the shutter button partially pressed, and aim at the scene you want. This will lock in the proper focus distance and ignore any interference that may lie between you and the subject.

Shooting in Locked Autofocus   Locked autofocus works well for almost every shooting situation. Here's how you use locked autofocus:

1. Check to see whether your camera lets you choose between locked autofocus and continuous autofocus. If it does, turn off continuous autofocus (or at least make sure continuous autofocus is not turned on).

2. Look through the viewfinder and align the focus/spot metering target on the object or scene you want to focus on.

3. Since the target is in the center of the frame, it may be necessary for you to lock the focus and move it to adjust your composition. If so, press the shutter release button halfway. A small motor in the camera moves the lens in response to input from the sensor until the targeted image is in focus.

4. While holding the shutter to maintain the lock, rotate the camera to frame the image as you want.

5. Press the shutter button completely to take the picture.

NOTE   *Most cameras provide continuous autofocus without saying so. As you move the target to other objects at greater or lesser distances, the camera will adjust the focus automatically. If you want to use continuous focus, all you have to do is not lock the focus. Just fully press the shutter release button to shoot.*

Focusing in Manual Mode   If you can't find anything in the shot to lock into focus, you can switch to manual focus mode and set the focus for the correct distance. Most cameras let you switch off autofocus and then choose a preset distance from the LCD menu or rotate the lens by hand.

NOTE   *If you're focusing manually by the menu method, you won't be able see focus corrections in the optical viewfinder. You will have to use the LCD.*

Cameras equipped with an electronic or through-the-lens (TTL—as is SLR, single-lens reflex) viewfinders will have a much easier time focusing in manual mode, because they display exactly what the lens is seeing and are much easier to view than an LCD in bright light conditions. A few higher-end SLR digital cameras let you focus manually the old-fashioned way: you twist the lens barrel while watching the focus change on the camera SLR viewfinder's ground glass.

1. On most digital cameras, you can go to the LCD menu and choose the manual focus option. This turns off the autofocus sensors.

2. Use the jog control to select your focus from a list on the LCD menu.

3. If you know the distance to the object you want to focus on, you can set that value and shoot.

4. If you're not sure whether you set the correct distance, switch the LCD out of menu mode and aim the camera at the subject. The only way you'll know if your focusing guess was right will be to view the LCD. If you're in bright sunlight, you'll need an LCD hood (such as one made by Hoodman; see Chapter 15), or you can just throw a jacket or a piece of dark cloth over your head and the camera.

Fixed Focus   Low-end cameras can have fixed lenses that are preset to a specific focal length. When you are using a camera like this you will have clear focus from a few feet away to infinity. Check your camera's specifications for the minimum distance. These cameras cannot focus for close-up shots and cannot adjust for depth-of-field. Fixed focus is designed to take a standard snapshot and to keep the cost of the camera low.

24. Use the Two Viewfinders

The viewfinder is the optical or electronic window that you look through to compose a shot. It is the connection between your eye and the camera's eye, so in that sense it is a very important device. Virtually all digital cameras have two viewfinders—some sort of optical or SLR viewfinder that you view by putting your eye up to a window, and the LCD preview monitor on the back of the camera.

What Types of Eyepiece Viewfinders Are Available?

Within the eyepiece category are three types—optical, electronic, and through-the-lens (TTL) viewfinders.

Optical Viewfinders   The optical viewfinder is the simplest and most error-prone of the three types of eyepieces. It is a separate optical device that gives you a view that's more or less parallel to the view the lens sees.

Because an optical viewfinder provides only a facsimile of the lens view, the closer your shot is to the camera the greater the offset between what the viewfinder sees and the framing of the photo that the camera would actually take at that moment. This disparity is technically known as *parallax error*. To ensure against accidental cropping due to parallax error, you should know that most optical viewfinders are designed to see about 85 percent of the total image area that will be recorded. You should accommodate for this. Most digital cameras that sell for under $1000 use optical viewfinders because they cost much less to build than TTL or electronic SLR viewfinders.

Try This: Learn to Compensate for Parallax

Take a photograph of something that has a uniform gridlike structure, such as a window with equal panes or a brick/cement block wall. Make a note of where you line up the edges when you look through the viewfinder. Take the shot. Look at the shot after you take it and you will clearly see how far the image shifted from where you lined it up. Take other test shots from closer and then farther away and you will see how the shift changes as you get closer and how it is diminished by distance. Familiarize yourself with the shift in your camera so you can compensate when shooting.

Optical viewfinders do have a couple of advantages: You can see what you're aiming at under any type of lighting conditions. They are also the preferred type of viewfinder for fast action because you can frame the picture quickly.

Figure 4-5 shows the disparity between what the viewfinder shows and what is actually captured in the photograph.

NOTE   *Optical viewfinders usually come with a diopter adjustment for photographers who wear glasses. This is a small dial next to the optical viewfinder that allows you to adjust the focus to compensate for your eyeglasses. They usually have a limited range and don't work for every case.*

Electronic Viewfinders   An electronic viewfinder is a step above an optical viewfinder because it more accurately shows you what the lens is seeing and doesn't result in parallax errors. It does this by placing a tiny LCD display within the eyepiece that gives you the same view as the standard LCD display. The size of the viewfinder dictates that it be fairly low resolution, so seeing minute detail can be a problem, especially when you're trying to focus manually. It also represents a power drain and will run down batteries quickly. On the other hand, if you are not using the larger LCD as a viewfinder, you are saving considerable battery power.

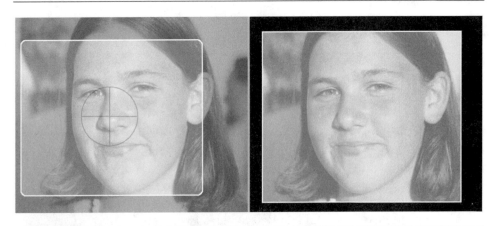

FIGURE 4-5   You can see the viewfinder view (left) and the obvious shift in the photograph (right).

Through-the-Lens Viewfinders   The TTL viewfinder is by far the best solution for accurate framing, because it allows you to view your shot through the lens itself. Found in traditional SLR cameras, TTL viewfinders use mirrors or prisms to divert the light passing through the main camera lens onto ground glass. A prism then inverts the picture to its normal orientation and you view it through an optical eyepiece.

This system is expensive and is found only on digital cameras in the $1000-plus consumer/professional price range.

What Types of LCD Viewfinders Are Available?

LCD viewfinders are found on all but the smallest and cheapest digital cameras. They are even beginning to show up on a few film cameras—proof that anybody can benefit from a good idea.

LCD monitors perform multiple tasks, one of which is to act as a viewfinder. The LCD display is basically a small laptop monitor located on the back of your camera that projects an accurate view of what your lens is seeing. The LCD provides the best approximation of how the final photograph will be framed, because it shows you the same picture that is recorded by the image sensor chip. The picture you see (provided it's not washed out by bright surrounding light or darkened by viewing it from an angle) is exactly how the sensor is interpreting the current camera settings. It's as if you've gotten the film back from the lab before you've even taken the picture—like having a darkroom with you in the field.

As for the drawbacks of LCD viewfinders, they are hard to see in bright light situations and they use a lot of power. If you are doing most of your shooting outdoors, get an LCD hood or carry around a square yard of black felt that you can throw over your head when it's critical to be able to prejudge exposure. Hopefully, somebody will find a way to make LCD displays usable in all lighting conditions, because they do provide some profound advantages over other types of viewfinders.

NOTE   *When you use your LCD monitor as your viewfinder, you must take extra precautions to steady your camera, because it is not braced against your cheek and because you are probably holding the camera with outstretched arms. Use higher shutter speeds if possible. Also, put the neck strap around your neck or chest and stretch it as tightly as possible with your arms. The tension takes away unsteadiness in your grip.*

How Do I Use the Different Viewfinders?

The following chart indicates the best use for each type of viewfinder. As you can see, the LCD is by far the most versatile.

Condition	Viewfinder Types			
	Optical	Electronic	TTL	LCD Display
Distant shots	X	X	X	X
Close shots		X	X	X
Need for accurate framing		X	X	X
Shooting angles that make looking through the eyepiece difficult				X
Candid shooting	X		X	
Stop action	X		X	
Need to see color cast				X
Need to see exposure settings				X
Need to see depth-of-field			X	X
Need to preview shots				X
Need to conserve power	X			
Reduce shutter lag	X			
Bright sunlight	X	X	X	
Low lighting	X		X	X
Normal lighting	X	X	X	X

25. Using the LCD in Bright Sunlight

The light used to illuminate LCDs is pretty weak and was originally designed to be used in controlled lighting conditions, which can be dimmed to make viewing the LCD easy. (For more information on LCDs, see Tip 7 in Chapter 2.)

Why Is Using the LCD in Sunlight an Issue?

Most of us have experienced the frustration of having surrounding bright light make it difficult to read an LCD display. Until the technology is improved so outside viewing is not a problem, you will need to use some shading device in bright conditions, or you have to use your optical viewfinder exclusively to frame shots. Although it's usually the other way around, some low-end cameras don't have viewfinders, so you are forced to use the LCD.

How Do I Set Up and Use the LCD in Sunlight?

An LCD could almost be a substitute for an SLR—if only you could see it in lighting conditions where it was bright enough to take a picture without supplemental lighting. Actually, all you need is a $2 handheld, plastic slide viewer or a nylon and Velcro accessory called the Hoodman, which sells for $20 (see Chapter 15). The Hoodman is also excellent protection for the LCD when the camera is in its carrying case. LCD hoods are also available through some camera manufacturers as accessories.

Finally, you could make your own hood device with a dollar's worth of black felt board, a straight edge, an Xacto knife, and some black masking tape. Or, the best device of all is to use a square yard (bigger is even better) of cheap black felt—just drape it over the camera and your head. You'll be able to see the LCD perfectly, but watch out for speeding cyclists (and unsolicited comments on your sense of fashion)!

26. Understand Metering Options

Photographs have *everything* to do with light. Light is what we are trying to capture and record on the image sensors in the most accurate manner possible. Light meters are designed to help you analyze the intensity, contrast, and even color of the light that is collected by the lens. This will allow you or the camera to set the exposure levels properly and capture as much detail as possible. Light meters are not a perfect science, although they are getting more sophisticated and accurate all the time. You should realize that no metering system is foolproof, and only experience and sometimes trial and error will prevail.

What Types of Light Meters Are Available?

Two types of light meters are available: *incident* and *reflective*. Incident light meters read the light inside of a frosted ball located within the meter, resulting in an accurate measure of the intensity of the light *falling onto* the subject, rather than the intensity of light *being reflected* from the subject. This is the best way to measure light so that objects that are predominantly lighter or darker than 50 percent gray (reflectively neutral) don't misguide the reading by fooling the meter into thinking that the overall scene is darker than it really is. Wise use of incident light meters takes some training and experience. You also need to hold the meter directly in front of the subject if you want to get the most accurate readings.

You'll encounter reflective meters much more frequently. Most of these are built into your camera. Many built-in meters read the light directly through the lens, which is the most accurate method. Some cameras have a separate miniature lens used by the built-in meter. Although these are generally okay, you should make sure that you don't cover the meter lens with your finger while you're shooting. Also, don't let it get struck by direct sunlight or your reading will be disastrously skewed.

When a reflected light meter is built into the camera, the camera's electronics use the exposure data generated by the meter to set the proper exposure (aperture and shutter speed) according to the other parameters you've set (such as bracketing settings).

A number of metering methods provide different results in various lighting conditions. Few cameras feature all these options, so refer to your camera's specifications to see which options are available with your camera.

Figure 4-6 shows how different light-metering systems analyze the area of the frame to determine the correct exposure.

Average Center Weighted Metering   The most common metering system in digital cameras, average center weighted metering takes 60 to 80 percent of the reading from the center third of the image. Its advantage is that it modifies the center readings with some averaged information about the rest of the scene. This type of metering assumes that the focal point of the scene is always at the center. This, of course, is seldom true. It works best if the camera lets you target what you want to get a reading on, lock it in, and then realign the shot. Because the target area is much more general than a spot meter, center weighted metering is more likely to be "good enough" when you don't have time to be accurate with where you aim it.

NOTE   *A few of the newest and most expensive professional 35mm SLR film cameras have meters that follow your eye in order to place the focus spot. You never have to reposition the camera. You can bet that eventually this technology will find its way onto digital cameras, but don't wait until then to buy one.*

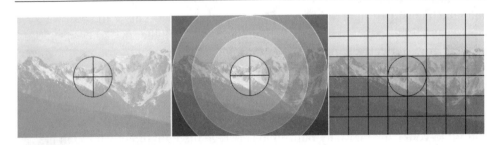

FIGURE 4-6   Common metering options, from left to right: spot, average center weighted, and matrix

Spot Metering   Spot metering takes the entire reading from a small circle—usually 3 to 15 percent of the entire image. Most cameras let you lock the spot meter in the same way you lock focus with a half shutter press. This allows you to take a reading, hold it, and then realign the shot. Spot metering lets you take readings on specific objects and ignore everything else. This guarantees that you get a good exposure on that targeted object, but it may result in unpredictable exposures in other parts of the scene. Because it ignores all but the most important area of the scene, spot metering is particularly appropriate for shots with back lighting, spot lighting, highly contrasting backgrounds (such as snow and black velvet), and macro shots. Spot meters require fairly accurate aiming, so you should be careful that you target an area that represents an average brightness of the subject.

NOTE   *You can't get built-in incident light meters, but you can get the same results by spot metering a matte-surfaced object that is 50 percent gray. You can buy 50 percent gray cards from any professional photographer's store for a few dollars.*

Matrix Metering   Matrix metering divides the scene into a number of grid segments (the number of segments varies with the type of camera) and calculates the brightness and contrast levels separately for each segment. The information about brightness and contrast is used to analyze the proper exposure based on a database of information derived from thousands of photographs and stored in the camera's computer memory. This advanced type of metering is good at avoiding extreme or unusual lighting conditions from being averaged into the exposure settings and throwing them off. It can decide when to discount the sky or a bright candle in a dark room, for example, and to guess at which areas are the most important in the picture—some cameras even let you pick which matrix areas to emphasize (a Nikon strong point). This is the most advanced type of metering.

Why Do I Need Metering Options?

Every metering option has strengths and weaknesses. Having options allows you to optimize the way you take light readings based on your shooting conditions. So far, no single metering method can provide a foolproof way of getting the exposure perfect every time. You will sometimes need to switch the way your camera takes readings if you want the greatest capability under all conditions. Advances are being made, and these point to a more advanced matrix system becoming the standard in cameras in the future.

How Do I Choose the Right Metering Option?

The camera you own will sometimes limit the type of metering options you have available. High-end cameras will almost always offer more options. Familiarize yourself with what your camera offers.

The matrix system offers the best all-around performance but is currently available only on high-end cameras. The low-range to midrange cameras will most likely have average center weighted and spot metering options, which work pretty well, especially since most digital cameras allow you to lock the meter target with the focus. Use the average center weighted method for conditions in which lighting is more evenly distributed and not too extreme. This will most likely be the default method for your camera, but check your manual to be sure. Use the spot meter method when you have a backlit subject, high-contrast lighting, or a macro shot—or when you want accurate incident light metering by reading a gray card or other neutral-brightness object (such as skin tones).

Remember the advantage of digital is that you have infinite test-shot capability, so if it's critical, take a few test shots for exposure. If the automatic metering is not providing what you want, use the exposure compensation or priority modes to correct it. With film, this is not so easy.

27. Keep It Steady

Steady in the world of photography is the relationship between the movement of the camera and the speed of the shutter. Keeping the camera steady means not letting it move at all while the shutter is open. And the slower the shutter speed, the stiller the camera needs to be.

Why Is Keeping It Steady Important?

If the movement of the camera is faster that the shutter speed, the image will be blurred (to put it another way, less than sharp). This effect is commonly called *camera motion blur*. Unlike the motion blur that results when the subject is moving too fast for the camera shutter to stop it, camera motion blur rarely produces a photograph that one would consider to be of acceptable quality.

How Do I Keep the Camera Steady in Different Situations?

The best way to keep your camera steady is to place it on a platform that is stable. A tripod is the most typical platform used by photographers, but single pole supports (called monopods) work well and are more compact and portable.

If a camera stand is not available, you can use any solid object with a flat surface large enough to accommodate the camera, such as a fence post, a rock, or your car.

Wind can often make it difficult to steady a camera, and it can knock a camera from a perch if the camera is not securely attached. If you are shooting with another person, your assistant can stand in a position to block the wind or hold up a windbreak of some sort. Another difficult situation is in crowds, where you may get nudged and jostled. Shoot with your back against a wall so you are not pushed from behind. Putting obstacles, like chairs or an assistant, around you can divert traffic momentarily while you take the shot. If you are the outgoing type, you can announce that you want to take a shot and people will sometimes stop to give you some elbow room (but that's an approach that often makes subjects self-concious when you're trying for spontaneity in a candid photo).

28. Make Test Shots

The test shot becomes the proving ground for your theories about how your photograph is going to look when you press that shutter release button. Never fear; you will find yourself getting it right more often as you get used to your camera and how to control it.

Why Should I Take Test Shots?

With digital cameras, test shots are totally painless, unless you are far from a store and dangerously low on battery power. Digital "film" can be used over and over, so you can take as many shots as you want without running to the store to buy film and waiting to get prints back.

The camera's LCD becomes your test track, and you can send images out for a spin as often as you like. If you don't like an image, you can just erase it and try again. Obviously this is not possible for every situation, but when you can, it is good practice to test your shots. Besides, the more you practice this way, the sooner your instincts will be able to take over and produce the results you want. When you are learning, test shots are an invaluable tool that can help you discover what you and your camera can do.

Those of us who are traditional photographers using mechanical cameras venture forth with the best of intentions, and then we forget to take notes to keep track of the settings we used for test shots. By the time the film comes back from the lab, we've forgotten all about what it took to get those shots. Once again, the digital camera comes to the rescue. Unbeknownst to many, most cameras automatically record just about everything you might care to know about how you shot any digital picture. This information is stored in something called an EXIF file, which is actually a small part of the data recorded into your camera's RAW, TIFF, or JPEG file. The image browser in the latest versions of Photoshop 7 and Elements 2.0 will automatically show you the EXIF information any time you select a file's thumbnail.

Figure 4-7 shows a series of test shots taken with various settings. Taking such test shots with various camera settings is called *bracketing* and is discussed in Tip 38 in Chapter 6.

How Do I Take a Test Shot?

If you're going to be making a critical shot or shooting a series of shots in the same situation, or if you have to shoot in other than average lighting conditions, you can take the shot, preview it on your LCD screen, and then adjust the exposure accordingly and reshoot.

With a digital photo, you should always expose for the highlights and then correct for the shadows later in an image editor. (See Tip 61 in Chapter 9 for more information.) Using the LCD as your viewfinder, you can also see the exposure settings change as you adjust them, to get a sense of the proper settings before you take the shot. This is a big advantage over a conventional mechanical camera. It is always a good idea to shoot a range of settings to have a basis for comparison and to understand more about the range of possibilities available. You may discover effects that you couldn't have guessed just by trying something a little out of the ordinary.

FIGURE 4-7   Which test shot would you choose as the keeper?

Chapter 5

Lighting Techniques

Photography is ultimately about understanding light. What we see and photograph is actually nothing more than the prevailing light that is reflected from the surfaces of the things around us. It is the color and intensity of that reflected light that forms the picture—both in our heads and in the camera. So obviously, becoming a master of controlling and capturing light is at the heart of good photography. In this chapter I will give you some insights into how to work with and control the lighting so that your camera can capture the best image possible. You will learn how to use available lighting and artificial lighting, and how to overcome some common problems associated with lighting. Learning good lighting techniques is a fundamental piece of knowledge that will set a solid foundation for your photographic endeavors.

29. Use the Built-in Flash

Almost all digital cameras come with an electronic flash that is built into the camera body and is triggered by the shutter release button. The flash is programmed to fire automatically when the light sensors indicate that available light is insufficient for a good exposure. You can also manually force it to fire or suppress it.

The flash is a strobe-type light and can be fired again and again as long as your camera has enough power. To achieve an appropriate level of exposure, the camera has to build up to a prescribed voltage. This eats battery power and forces you to wait while the charge is being renewed before you can take the next shot. A light indicator near the eyepiece tells you when the flash has power and is ready to fire again. If you are planning to use your flash a lot, it's wise to have extra batteries or an external battery pack, or be connected to an AC adapter that's plugged in.

If it's the only light source, the built-in flash is better than nothing—and at least you'll be able to get the picture—but the direction of the flash's light can't be controlled by the photographer, and it usually produces unflattering shadows and overbright highlights. Flash has limited range and cannot get you a reasonable exposure of anything much farther away than 10 to 12 feet. The cure is easy and can cost you less than $100: Buy an automatic external flash that is brighter than the internal flash. (See the next tip in this chapter for more information on using external flashes.)

Why Do I Need to Use a Built-in Flash?

Almost any situation in which flash is needed or desired can be better served by an external flash than an internal flash. There are, however, two exceptions: fill flash and the times when the built-in flash is the only choice you have.

Fill Flash   One of the best uses for built-in flash is for shooting pictures (especially of people) in bright sunlight. This is called a *fill flash* because it helps reduce the harsh contrast of direct sunlight by filling in shadow with light. The result is a more evenly exposed image. When using the built-in flash as a fill, the existing light will have to be brighter than the flash. Since the camera is ordinarily programmed to use the flash only when the lack of available light leaves you no other choice, you will have to use a setting that forces the flash to fire under any conditions. It's even better if your camera has a fill flash setting, because the camera will then use the brightness of the existing light as a gauge for how bright the flash fill should be and will automatically set the flash accordingly.

Dim or Dark Lighting Conditions   Built-in flashes are used when not enough light is available to get a good exposure. In low light conditions, the camera will automatically kick in the flash to compensate if it cannot find an exposure setting that will work with available light. If you don't want the flash to fire in these conditions, you will need to suppress it manually. Generally, this is a matter of toggling a flash button on the camera so that the flash symbol changes on the control panel LCD.

Fill flash   No flash

When Time Is of the Essence   Some shots do not leave you any time to set up or experiment with a flash. This is when you will want to use the camera in full automatic mode and let it do the best it can—with or without automatic flash. With more time, you might do better, but if you need the photo as a record, a shot produced in this way is better than no shot at all.

Nighttime Shots   Remember that the flash has a limited range, so if you're taking night shots, be aware that the background beyond the flash range will appear black, as shown in Figure 5-1. On many cameras, the flash has a "slow" mode that can be used for properly exposing night shots by freezing the subject with flash while using slow shutter speed to bring out the background with a longer exposure. (See Tip 31, later in this chapter.) Unless you intentionally want to blur the background as an effect, use a tripod.

FIGURE 5-1   This is a good use of an internal flash where the moment was at hand and light was limited.

Moving Objects in Low Light   Capturing moving objects requires a fast shutter speed, so you will need a fair amount of available light to allow such a shutter speed. In low light conditions, the flash will stop the action at close range. The flash is a valuable tool for journalists and close-up nature photographers, for instance. If you have to use the built-in flash as the only light source for subjects more than ten (or so) feet away, raise the ISO rating in your camera. You'll find that adjustment in your camera's LCD menu. Each doubling of the ISO rating will add about five feet to your maximum range.

How Do I Set Up and Use the Built-in Flash?

The camera's default is to put the flash in auto flash mode, so that every time you partially press the shutter button (which turns on the light meter), the sensors are reading the available light and determining whether the flash should fire. If you have set the camera so that the flash will fire, an indicator will tell you when the flash is ready. If you shoot before you get that signal, it's likely that your flash will underexpose the subject. The camera will also determine the brightness and/or the duration of the flash based on the autofocus distance from the subject. In auto flash mode, this indicator will work only when the light levels are low enough to require the flash.

The following camera settings (modes) determine whether the flash fires and how the flash calculates its duration (exposure).

Auto Flash   The camera defaults to this setting. To switch back to auto flash mode from another flash mode, press the flash mode button on your camera until the appropriate symbol is displayed on the control panel.

Fill Flash   Fill flash is a useful option (but fairly rare) that's well worth looking for. Press the flash mode button until the fill flash symbol appears on the control panel. In this mode, the flash will fire regardless of available light, and it will be adjusted to be a lower intensity flash so it doesn't overpower available light. This is the subtle but important difference between a fill flash setting and a forced on setting. Set your metering target on the subject in the shadow and lock it to get a proper exposure with a half press of the shutter.

An example of what the fill flash can do is shown in Figure 5-2.

Red-Eye Reduction   Press the flash mode button until the red-eye reduction symbol appears in the control panel. In this mode, a short flash will fire ahead of the shutter release to reduce the effect of red eye. (For more information, see Tip 33, later in this chapter.)

NOTE   *Image-editing software will do a far better job of red-eye reduction than the camera will. In fact, I'd suggest not using the camera's red-eye reduction feature at all. It works by firing a preflash that causes the subject's pupils to shrink. It also causes the subject to blink and causes external slave flashes to fire at the wrong time.*

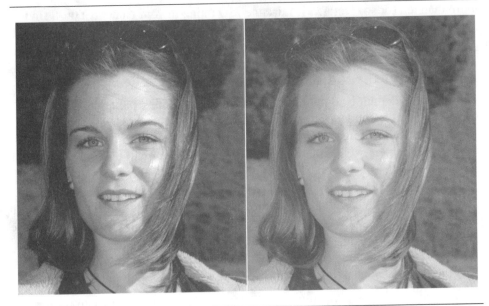

FIGURE 5-2   You see how well the shadows were balanced with the high contrast light on this subject by using a fill flash (right), as opposed to the photo with no fill (left).

Slow Synchronization   This mode will give you a more balanced exposure between foreground and background in night shots. Check your camera's manual to determine how to set slow sync flash. (It is usually set on the LCD menu.) You will want to steady the camera on a stable object or tripod before you shoot, as the slow shutter speed will cause the background to blur if the camera isn't rock steady. (For more information, see Tip 31 later in this chapter.)

Try This: The Kleenex Cure for an Internal Flash

If your camera doesn't have a fill flash setting, you can tape a layer or two of Kleenex or use a neutral-density filter over the flash so that the actual brightness of the flash will be a stop or two lower than the camera calculates. The Kleenex trick has the added advantage of diffusing the light from the fill flash—and is a good idea for indoor candid photos. If you use it indoors, you'll need to compensate for slight underexposure when you process the image in your image editor, which you can do with an auto-correct command in a single button-click.

Off   Press the flash mode button until the manual off symbol appears in the control panel. In this mode, the flash is prevented from firing. This is good for situations in which you don't want a flash even in low light because:

- You'd rather risk a little blur or ISO-boost noise than lose the atmosphere provided by available light.

- You want to reduce shutter lag.

- Battery power is low.

- Flashes are prohibited.

Sometimes shooting with natural light is the only way to go, even if it's a low light situation. If you want to convey a cozy mood like the one shown in Figure 5-3, for example, you wouldn't want the flash to brighten up the picture too much.

FIGURE 5-3   Natural lighting is often the best way to capture the subtleties of mood.

30. Use an External Flash

It's a good idea to use an external flash in addition to or instead of your built-in flash. The external flash can be connected to your camera via a hot shoe, a sync cord, or a *slave* unit (an electronic sensor that fires the flash it's attatched to when it sees the flash from another unit or receives a radio signal). It can attach to the camera with a mounting bracket, or it can be handheld or mounted on a separate stand. If you don't have experience with using external flashes, start with an inexpensive one that features automatic exposure calculation and a built-in slave unit. Sunpak and Vivitar (among others) make units that sell for less than $100.

The advantages of the built-in slave control is that you don't need cords, so you don't have to worry about the sync cord pulling the flash or the camera to the pavement if a passerby happens to bump into it.

Why Do I Need to Use an External Flash?

An external flash is superior to a built-in flash in every way except cost and portability. The external flash

- Makes it possible to bounce light, scattering it so that it can illuminate a much larger area evenly and greatly soften the edges of shadows.

- Illuminates a much larger area, which will extend the depth of your shot.

- Eliminates red eye because it doesn't fire directly into the subject's pupils. (See Tip 33, later in this chapter.)

- Makes it possible to use multiple external flashes so that you can light several areas of the photo (for example, background and foreground) at once. This is almost imperative if you have to shoot crowds, events, or interiors.

How Do I Set Up and Use an External Flash?

Attach the external flash to your camera via the sync cord or the hot shoe, depending on what's available with your camera. Some flash units have a mounting bracket that attaches to the mounting screw on the bottom of the camera. If you're using a flash with a built-in meter, the flash will calculate its own exposure, even if you bounce or diffuse it. If you use a significantly more expensive unit that receives instructions from your camera, the flash exposure setting will be set through the camera's built-in meter, which can be even more accurate.

Your camera should be set to aperture-priority mode and to the manufacturer's recommended aperture for your external flash. For even more control over exposure, you can set your flash and camera to manual mode and calculate detailed settings for your shot.

If you use a slave-style flash, make sure the slave unit is positioned to see the primary flash. If you use a built-in slave that faces forward, you may need to use a small pocket mirror to catch the light from the primary (cue) and bounce it back into the slave sensor. When using an external flash, the internal flash can serve as a fill. If you don't want the internal flash to serve as a fill, you'll need at least one external flash that is hard-wired to the camera. The hard-wired external flash either can be your sole light (which can be bounced for broader, softer coverage) or can serve as the cue light for another, slave-fired, external flash.

A number of common external flash configurations will be useful in most shooting situations:

- Handheld portrait (an arm's length away, at a 45-degree angle from the camera). This can also be used in conjunction with the built-in fill flash to soften shadows.

- Bounced off a white wall, ceiling, or card to provide general, natural looking lighting for large areas.

- As a key light with the built-in flash used as fill. The key light is the dominant light sources. Two light sources are usually better than one. A second flash or other light source will dramatically increase your ability to control the contrast of the light and produce properly contoured objects with good detail in the shadows.

Try This: Turn Your Internal Flash into an Invisible Remote

You can hide the light from the internal flash and still use it to fire a slave unit. Just tape a piece of fully exposed and developed color transparency film over the built-in flash's lens. The flash will then transmit only invisible infrared light, which happens to be visible to slave sensors. This is a great way to use external flashes with cameras that don't have any kind of connector for an external flash.

NOTE

Most digital camera flash connectors are made to be used with flashes that are manufactured specifically for one brand or range of cameras. Camera manufacturers generally make their connectors so that they will work only with their own brands of flash, which, of course, cost about twice as much as generic automatic external flashes. Because camera-specific flashes are often made to set themselves according to a meter reading taken through the camera's lens or sensor, they tend to be more accurate than the generic models. However, the generic models I've tested from Sun and Vivitar have proven to be amazingly accurate, extremely easy to use, and affordable, and they have built-in slave sensors.

31. Keep the Background Bright and Naturally Lit with Slow Sync Flash

This is a function of the built-in flash and has everything to do with timing. When selected, the slow sync flash will go off early in a long exposure shot to illuminate nearby objects while letting background areas expose at a slower rate, which helps balance the overall exposure. The flash is synchronizing with the total exposure time by firing selectively at the start or end of the time exposure shot. It is designed to help you take better shots in low light conditions. It can also produce unique blurring effects on moving objects with lights at night.

Why Do I Need to Use Slow Sync Flash?

One of the problems with using flash, especially if it's built-in, is that anything more than a couple of feet behind the subject tends to look very dark in the shot. If you're shooting outdoors (especially at night), the background will simply go black.

Figure 5-4 shows an example of this. The picture on the left is a slow sync shot. The image on the right was shot with a straight flash.

How Can I Use Slow Sync Flash to Improve the Exposure?

You can work around the problem of dark backgrounds when using the flash in low light by keeping the shutter open long enough to expose the background properly to bring it into view.

The camera should be mounted on a tripod to keep it steady during the long exposure times. The flash will fire when the shutter is released, but the shutter will remain open for a bit longer.

FIGURE 5-4   You can see a lot more detail behind the foreground figures in the slow sync shot on the left, as opposed to the blacked-out background on the right.

32. Lighting Portraits

A portrait photograph is a photograph with one or two people as its primary focal point or predominant subject. An example of a portrait is shown in Figure 5-5.

Why Do I Need Special Lighting for People?

The human eye and brain are particularly sensitive to the physical details of people images, so it's worth your time to take extra care when photographing people so they look "real" (if that's the look you want). For example, if skin tones or hair colors are off, the whole perception of the subject is affected, because our powerful preconceived image of what people are supposed to look like takes over.

The human form is complex and has many shapes, colors, and textures that reflect light and cast shadows in varying ways. Getting the reflection in someone's glasses to disappear or eliminating red eye requires special lighting.

Try This: See It Now or See It Later?

Some cameras allow you to set a slow sync flash to go off at either the beginning or the end of the longer exposure. Each produces a different blurring effect on moving objects. Experiment with it and see which one you prefer.

FIGURE 5-5   An example of a well-lit portrait

Portrait photography is particularly demanding, because you are "freezing" the subject at a particular point in time. Most of us rarely sit as still as we appear in a portrait. In addition, we viewers don't normally stare at people—as we do at a portrait. It's impolite, for one thing. Part of the fascination of portrait photography is that we can stare at it and see every detail. This is why detail in the picture must be as exceptional as it can be. Lighting plays a key role in that endeavor.

Lighting can also be used to indicate a person's mood, environment, and even emotion. For example, taking a picture in the early morning when the sun is weak can produce a cool light that will give the effect of a cool environment. Put that together with a person bundled in warm clothing, and you have a convincing cool-weather shot, even though it may have been taken in August.

How Do I Set Up and Use Lighting to Improve Portrait Photos?

In outdoor settings, soft diffused light is best—it reduces the effect of harsh shadows because the light is scattered, much like the effect of a lampshade or a frosted bulb. Get into shooting in shade or shoot on cloudy days. North light (indirect sunlight) is ideal. Try to shoot at the beginning and end of the day if you can. Face the subject so that the light is coming from behind the camera (avoiding backlighting). If you must shoot in bright sunlight, check out the sections on using fill flash in Tip 29 at the beginning of this chapter.

If you're shooting indoors, you can use a main light (a key light) that is roughly 1/3 brighter than the fill light. You generally want this light to be located about a foot above the camera and a foot to the left for glamour portraits, and higher and further to the left for more traditional portraits. We read from left to right so our eyes tend to move naturally in that direction and follow the light. Use a second light for fill. Diffuse light sources are generally better for shooting women and older people (for softer contouring of features and minimization of wrinkles and eye bags). Use higher contrast lighting for men and for characters (for a more angular, hard-edged rendering of features).

33. Control Red Eye

When the pupils in someone's eyes appear unnaturally red in the photograph, it is referred to as *red eye*.

Why Does Red Eye Occur?

Red eye occurs when you use a straight-on flash, such as a built-in flash. The light actually goes into the pupil of the subject's eye and bounces off the retina and back into the camera lens after being tinted red by the blood in the eye. (Pretty gross, huh?)

How Do I Minimize Red Eye in My Photos?

Most digital cameras have a red-eye reduction mode. It works by firing a preflash to cause the subject's pupils to get smaller in reaction to the initial bright light, so that there's less chance of reflecting light from the back of the eyeball during the actual flash. This technique works, but it causes a couple of undesirable problems:

■ The preflash causes the subject to blink, and the end of the blink, when the eyes are reopening, occurs just when the real flash occurs and the shutter clicks. So the subject looks drugged, because the eyelids are half open.

■ This kind of shot increases shutter lag by a factor of two to three, because the camera has to wait for the preflash to complete before the flash and the shutter can fire—so you almost always miss the critical moment.

Your best bet is to turn off red-eye reduction and fix the red eyes in your image editor. The exception, of course, is when you're making shots that you want to transmit immediately to another source or place on the Web.

34. Use Reflectors to Fill in Shadows in Sunlight

An alternative to using fill flash when you're shooting portraits or still lifes in bright sunlight is to use a reflector to bounce light from the sun back into the shadow areas. You can use any white or silver reflecting surface. Reflectors are much better than fill flash for filling shadows in indirect lighting, such as shady situations or cloudy days.

A reflector is any surface that bounces light. Light, neutral-colored surfaces, preferably smooth white or silver, do the best job of reflecting light. Foam board is readily available in art supply stores and is often used for that purpose. Another readily available and portable reflector is one of the folding reflectors that are used to keep the temperature down in parked cars (also a good idea for protecting your camera gear from extreme temperatures when it's locked in the car). The metallic car reflectors are very bright.

Try This: A Good Reflection on Your Photos

Try using the folding reflector that you place in your car windshield for a reflector. They're sold at flea markets for next to nothing. Some come with a different color on each side, so you can create effects by bouncing a blue or gold light from the reflector into the shadow areas. Try projecting reflected light through different kinds of translucent or perforated material to get patterns of light effects.

Why Do I Need to Use a Reflector to Light a Scene?

When photographing in bright sunlight, you can often get harsh shadows in your shot. Reflected light can provide another light source to help mitigate this harsh shadow effect. Reflected light can also be used as a special effect to increase shadow effects or to cast another colored light on a subject. Reflectors are much better than fill flash for filling shadows in contrasting lighting, but not as easy to manage without a helper. In indirect lighting, such as shade or cloudy days, reflectors are the only affordable and portable way to fill shadows.

How Do I Set Up and Use Reflectors?

Positioning is the key to making reflected light work properly. The reflectors need to be facing into the sun at an angle that bounces the light back at the subject. It helps if you have a friend along to hold the reflector. You can also use light reflected off existing structures, such as a white building wall, a white sand beach, or water. The most important factors to watch out for in positioning reflectors are

- Don't position the reflector so close or use one that's so bright it causes cross shadows.

- Try to avoid shining into the subject's eyes, which may cause squinting.

- Don't aim it directly at the camera or you risk having it shown in the background or creating unwanted lens flare.

- Don't position it so that its light casts a shadow on the subject.

35. Use Inexpensive Lighting for Extreme Close-ups (Macros)

When shooting extreme close-ups (also known as *ECUs* or *macros*), you often want to be able to control the direction and brightness of the light so that you can shoot at a small enough aperture to give you maximum depth-of-field.

How Do I Set Up and Use the Lighting to Optimize Close-ups?

The lights need to be placed fairly close to the subject at angles that won't reflect directly back into the lens. If the subject has shiny surfaces, be aware of how those surfaces are picking up the light. Don't position the lighting gear in such a way that the lighting equipment's mirrored image is reflected from the surface of a shiny subject and is seen by the camera.

Lights can get hot, so if your subject is sensitive to heat, you can either move your lights to a safe distance or turn them on only for the time it takes to actually shoot the picture. Finally, be sure your camera isn't so close to the subject that it casts shadows on the subject. If that's the case, move the lights.

Try This: Available Lighting

The household-variety reflector flood lamps with frosted lenses can be placed into any standard lighting sockets and perform fairly well as close-up lights. Gooseneck floor lamps make affordable light stands for these lamps. If color accuracy is important to you, visit your local photo store and buy blue lamps that have been prebalanced for daylight. This will help you shoot in a room with lots of window light. If you want a soft light source for still-life subjects, make a tent from a clear frosted shower curtain liner, or better, use flexible frosted sheets of plastic and then shine the lamps through the tent. You can also use light diffusers that are made for ceiling fluorescent lights.

Lighting is also important in bringing out surface texture, which can be one purpose of shooting extreme close-ups. Getting the light angled to cast shadows that accentuate the surface can produce a much more dramatic image, as you can see in Figure 5-6. Macro images can also be backlit to produce a glowing effect, like sun through the petals of a flower or an ice crystal pattern on a window.

FIGURE 5-6   The effect of proper lighting on a macro shot

Chapter 6

Overcoming Difficult Situations

In the course of shooting you will come across situations that demand extra knowledge and experience to deal with them properly. Previously you may have passed up shooting in these situations because it seemed too daunting. Now it is time to break into some new territory. In this chapter I will give you some inside information on how to deal with those shots that take a bit more thought to capture but are really not that difficult once you know how to make your camera do the work. Freezing fast action, creating power motion effects, and shooting at night are all within your reach.

36. Freeze Fast Action

The terms *freeze* and *stop action* in photography refer to a single-frame photo that captures a clear image out of a sequence of motion. So much of modern life occurs in fast motion—cars, sports, people all hurrying about in the course of a day. If you want to capture clear images of life in motion, such as the image shown in Figure 6-1, your camera's shutter speed needs to be fast enough to capture the subject before it moves any perceptible distance or the image will be blurred. The faster the subject is moving, the faster the camera shutter needs to open and close to freeze it in motion.

FIGURE 6-1   You can "freeze" activities in a photograph that you might never get a good look at in real life.

Why Do I Need to Freeze Moving Subjects?

You need to learn how to shoot to freeze motion so you don't end up with blurry action shots. Freeze motion shots can be dynamic and exciting and are definitely a step up from static snapshots. Because you don't have much time to pose action shots, you need to be prepared to capture the perfect shot when it happens. This is a "get-it-while-you-can" mode, so learning how to be in the right place at the right time with the right settings is the name of the game.

How Do I Set Up the Camera to Take Fast Moving Shots?

The faster the shutter speed, the faster the action you will be able to stop. With a traditional camera, shutter speeds of 1/250 and 1/500 of a second are typically used to freeze a shot. With a high-end digital camera, you can shoot at speeds as fast as 1/5000 of a second. That is fast enough to stop a bullet midflight. More typically, 1/1000 of a second is considered very fast.

To set up a camera to freeze a shot, adjust the mode switch and LCD menu to put the camera in shutter-priority mode. Otherwise, the camera may make the correct exposure but choose a shutter speed that is too slow to stop the baseball or the ski jumper. Using the jog control and/or the mode dial, set the shutter at its fastest available speed—usually 1/500 of a second or greater. You should be able to see the shutter speed on the control panel at or near the top of your camera.

Take a test shot if you can, to determine whether the shutter speed you set eliminates blurring in the shot. If you can't get a proper reading at the highest shutter speed, increase the camera's ISO setting on the LCD menu. This is the equivalent of loading faster film in a conventional camera. If you still can't get the shot without blurring, use a flash—preferably an external flash (because they're brighter and you can determine the angle of light). It is best to mount the flash on a bracket attached to the camera so that it will follow the motion of the subject as you move the camera. If you use an external flash in otherwise dim lighting conditions (rather than as fill flash), you don't need to worry about the shutter speed—the duration of all electronic flash units is typically somewhere between 1/1000 and 1/10,000 of a second, which is faster than any shutter.

Shoot at the peak of the action—when the subject is moving the least and the shot looks the most exciting. If you have to choose, exciting is better than slow. Take a number of shots in sequence to maximize your chances of getting the best shot.

Make sure your camera is set for autofocus. If your camera has a continuous autofocus option (a special focus ability that lets you focus on-the-fly as images are changing), use it. If not, don't partially press the shutter button before you shoot or you'll lock focus on the subject before it reaches the point at which you want to take the picture. If the subject is moving toward or away from you, locking the focus will focus on the wrong spot, as the subject will have moved out of range.

37. Follow Motion to Blur the Background

Motion blur is the effect caused by moving the camera so the image is blurred on the image sensors. It is often the result of jittery camera handling on slower shutter speeds, but motion blur can have dramatic results when it's used intentionally with moving subjects.

Why Would I Want to Blur My Photograph?

Ideal subjects for a motion-blurring technique could be a coasting cyclist or skateboarder, a moving car, or a jet. Your objective in such a shot is to get the background to blur while keeping the focal point subject in sharp focus. This creates a visual illusion of the subject in motion that is more believable than just a freeze frame (see the previous tip). You can also use the inverse—freeze the background and let the moving subject blur. The resulting shot has a ghostly feel to it.

Figure 6-2 shows the motion-blurred scenery behind the person in a moving car.

FIGURE 6-2   The effect of motion blur accentuates the feeling of motion.

How Do I Use the Camera to Achieve This Effect?

Using a high shutter speed isn't the only way to freeze the target in motion—especially if that motion is primarily progressing across the image plane and isn't complex, like leaping in the air, twirling, or rapidly moving toward and away from you.

Shoot through the viewfinder, use continuous autofocus if it's available, and keep the focus target aligned with a specific feature of the subject, such as an article of clothing, so you can track it as you move the camera. Move the camera in a way that precisely follows the motion of the subject, keeping the camera's viewfinder aligned so that the subject maintains a constant position relative to the frame.

To get a smooth motion, you can use a panhead tripod. This is a tripod with a horizontally swiveling head that allows you to swivel the camera fluidly to follow motion, while other camera motion is locked in place. If you are going to shoot by hand, you can hold your arms rigidly next to your body while swiveling your torso to pan the shot. This will minimize vertical movement. You can also shoot from a moving vehicle that is pacing alongside a subject. (Make sure someone else is driving, of course, or you may be taking dramatic vehicle accident photos for the evening news!)

Motion blur can also be achieved in the inverse by setting your shutter speeds slower than 1/60 of a second so that the static background will be in sharp focus while the subject that is moving blurs.

You can also add motion blur later in image-editing programs (see Chapter 9).

38. Take Night Shots

A night shot is taken in dark conditions, such as outside in the evening or at night, in a dark room, or in a subway or other dark place. What I'm referring to as a night shot applies to any situation that has unusually low levels of light rather than the time of day. Taking a picture in a dark cave poses demands similar to those for taking pictures outside at night. Nighttime shooting conditions could actually be brightly lit or have high degrees of contrast—such as fireworks, nighttime sporting events, or city traffic.

Figure 6-3 is a shot that conveys the fantasy feeling of lights at night. Capture the urban world at night to produce some rewarding photographs.

Why Take Shots at Night?

Half (or more) of our lives takes place after the sun goes down, and some of the most exciting images are revealed at night. This is the mysterious time when people celebrate and socialize. This is also the time that architecture and the natural environment come alive with amazing displays of shadow and light. Some of the most dramatic photographs are taken in low light conditions, so learning to take night shots will expand your repertoire significantly.

FIGURE 6-3   Night shots can be taken at night in urban settings to capture a moment.

How Do I Take Night Shots?

You can shoot photos in the dark in two ways: with artificial light and with available light. Artificial lighting most typically involves using a flash or multiple flash units. It may also involve setting up key lights to illuminate certain parts of the scene. This tip focuses on shooting with available light, as flash shooting is covered in Chapter 5.

A Sturdy Tripod or Support Is Essential   When shooting at night with available light, you need to keep the camera steady. Because of the limited light, you will need to take *time exposures,* which involve keeping the shutter open for extended periods of time to gather more light—from a fraction of a second to a minute or more. The camera needs to be absolutely still during these long exposures, and this is impossible to do without a tripod or other steady camera support.

The Best Time to Shoot   Dusk, dawn, or in full moonlight, when there's a good balance between ambient (the general atmospheric light) and artificial lighting, make for some of the best shooting times. The darker the whole scene, the longer the exposure time necessary, which increases the possibility of movement in the scene, which produces streaks and blurs (although sometimes these can contribute interestingly to a night shot). Shooting in darkness will also tend to overexpose any bright lights. Early evening shots, like those shown in Figure 6-4, can produce dramatic results.

FIGURE 6-4   The moon's reflection illuminates the water and adds a whole new dimension (left), while early evening provides a backdrop for detail and good contrast for the lights (right).

You can capture a more evenly exposed scene at dusk and then darken it later with image-editing software much more effectively (see Chapter 9) than you can on the spot with your camera. In fact, you can even turn daylight photos into nighttime shots by manipulating an image with software. Don't boost your camera's ISO, because that increases image noise (graininess). Long exposures will also increase image noise. It is possible to eliminate some of this noise after the fact, but only by using professional image-editing software such as Photoshop 7 and specialized third-party programs.

Setting the Proper Exposure   Place your camera in spot meter mode if it's available, and half press the shutter release button to lock in a reading from the part of the image where you want to capture the most detail. This is especially important if you want detail in the brightest objects, such as a full moon or the detail inside a lighted building at night.

If you don't have a spot meter mode, zoom to telephoto, aim at the most important part of the scene, and half press the shutter release button to lock the reading. Then note the shutter speed and aperture displayed on the LCD and write down these settings. Switch to manual mode and set the shutter speed and aperture as you noted. Because you are shooting in manual mode, the settings won't change when you compose your shot.

If your camera doesn't have a manual mode, you can try a technique called *bracketing*.

1. Place the camera on a tripod. With the camera in autofocus mode, lock in your focus and meter, compose it, and take the picture.

2. Without changing modes, proceed to take several more pictures while using the jog control to adjust the exposure value (EV) to −.5, −1, +.5, and +1.

3. Preview the shots as you take them and discard those that don't work.

4. Keep adjusting the EV as necessary to get a good exposure.

Many digital cameras have a function called auto-bracketing, which will automatically take two extra pictures of both a higher and lower EV value in addition to the original shot. You can set this mode from the LCD menu. Use a slow sync flash to balance the exposure of background and foreground in night shots (see Chapter 5). If you bracket night shots with the camera on a tripod, you will be able to use parts of all three exposures when you are working in an image editor that supports layers, such as Photoshop Elements, Paint Shop Pro, or PictureIt!

39. Steady Handheld Shots in Dim Light

Handheld shots refer to shots taken while holding your camera in your hands instead of mounting it on a tripod or other device. You are the support for the camera while the shot is being taken.

Why Is It Important to Keep It Steady?

Unless you like blurry photographs, keeping the camera steady is essential to clear, sharp images. This is especially true in low light conditions when you are working with slower shutter speeds. Most photographers cannot hold a camera completely motionless. This is not a problem as long as the shutter speeds are above 1/60 of a second. If you are steady as a rock, you might be able to shoot down to 1/30, but at that speed the slightest breeze or nervous jitter will cause the camera to move and blur the image.

As mentioned earlier, blurring shots can create exciting and provocative photographs, but sometimes blurring just looks bad, as the shot in Figure 6-5 demonstrates.

FIGURE 6-5   Bracing the camera on the shoulder of the person nearby might have saved this shot.

How Do I Take a Good Handheld Shot in Dim Light?

You will often find yourself in situations in which the light levels fall and you don't have your tripod on hand. The first order is to set the shutter speed as high as you can by using aperture-priority mode; set it to fully open. If you are still in the danger zone, try looking for something you can use to brace the camera against—like a tree limb, fence post, or even your car. Any solid object will do.

Rest the camera on the object and set up your shot. With some type of support, you can adjust your camera's shutter and aperture to take the best shot. I have even used the back of a companion when I had to! Bean bags (any fabric sack filled with styrofoam pellets) will let you level the camera when bracing it on a slanted or irregularly shaped support, such as a banister or car hood.

If you are absolutely in a pinch and can't find anything to assist you, try using this stance to get as steady as you can: Kneel down with one knee on the ground and place the elbow of the arm holding the camera on the raised knee as support. This gives you a direct line of support to the ground and takes the weight off the arm. It isn't too comfortable, but it works. Or, if you want to add an unusual point of view (or if your subject is a child or pet), lie down in the prone rifle position that is used by so many sharpshooters to steady their aim.

Chapter 7

Things You Don't Do with Your Film Camera

The invention of digital technology has opened the door to new functionality never imagined in the days of conventional photography. Today's digital cameras can perform a wide range of tasks giving you a creative freedom that is really quite astounding. All packed in this marvelous little box of electronics is the ability to take 360-degree panoramic shots, create animation, and even shoot video clips, in addition to the traditional single-shot function. This chapter takes a closer look at this bag of tricks.

40. Make Panoramas

A panoramic shot is made up of a number of photographs that, when combined using specialized software, take in a wider or taller view than you could with a single normal-sized shot. The sequence of photographs is pieced back together into one larger picture using a software technique called *stitching*. In motion pictures, *panning* means moving the camera in a continuous motion from side to side or up and down to give the viewer a broader view of the scene. You are doing essentially the same thing with a sequence of stills when you take a panoramic shot.

Why Do I Need Panoramic Shots?

The process of panoramic shooting allows you to broaden your photographic horizons, literally. You can capture the expansiveness of the central plains, a magnificent city skyline, a complete shot of the world's tallest tree, or that endless stretch of shoreline. It is even possible to capture a 360-degree view. Figure 7-1 shows the difference between a regular shot and a panoramic shot.

When you look through your viewfinder, you'll notice that your view of the scene is limited only to what your lens can see. This is often disconcerting, because your eyes' peripheral vision is always much broader than the camera's. Of course, you can always pull back as far as the next county, but that shot won't show much detail. What do you do when you want to be closer and still get the whole vista in the picture? Creating a panoramic shot is the answer.

How Do I Set Up and Take a Panoramic Shot?

To shoot a panoramic sequence, you will need to overlap your shots, maintain a consistent focus distance from the subject in all your shots, keep the camera level, maintain a constant exposure from shot to shot, and transfer the images to a computer for merging into a panorama.

FIGURE 7-1   The view with a normally framed shot (top) and the same view shot as a panorama (bottom)

Overlap Your Shots   Shoot a number of pictures whose frames overlap by at least 30 percent—that is, the last 30 percent of the shot you just took should be the first 30 percent of the next shot, and so on. Try to find visual reference points before you shoot to guide you in overlapping the next shot. This will also give you cues to help you piece together the shot later when you're using image-editing software. Although the number of pictures you take is not fixed, some software applications have memory limitations regarding panorama merging, so don't take more shots than you need to cover your subject with the proper overlap. Some cameras have a panoramic mode, which will show you overlap guides on the LCD.

Maintain a Consistent Focal Distance   It's important that you keep the camera the same focal distance from your subject so that the perspective and proportions remain constant from shot to shot. Do not use the zoom lens or change the camera's position or center of rotation until the sequence of shots is complete. Be aware of moving subjects, especially when they are in the overlap area. If the subject is in the overlapping part of one frame and not the adjacent frame, it will confuse the stitching software.

Keep It Level   Keep the camera on a level track as you move through the sequence to make it easier to fit the pictures together with a minimum amount of distortion. The easiest way to do this is to use a tripod with a rotating head. Some come with degree markings that let you be precise. In the absence of a tripod, try to find a visual cue to guide you through the sequence, such as a horizon line. In fact, if you don't have a tripod, you're probably not going to get an acceptable stitch because very little affordable stitching software is good enough to "second-guess" the lack of consistency in camera position and rotational axis.

NOTE   *The most seamless panoramas are those shot by mounting the camera on a special tripod rig that rotates the camera about its absolute optical axis, which is usually somewhat in front of the camera's tripod thread—in fact, about halfway between the front element of the lens and the image sensor (digital "film"). It also helps to have a system for rotating the camera when it's set in a vertical orientation and a way of moving it in exact degrees of rotation. Several manufacturers make affordable versions of such rigs for a variety of digital cameras. The best known of these manufacturers is Kaidan.*

Maintain a Constant Exposure   If you are using a camera with automatic exposure, it will read and adjust the exposure with every shot. In a panoramic shot, you want to maintain a constant exposure to eliminate mismatches in color and brightness from one frame to another. You should use manual mode and lock in the exposure for all the shots in the sequence. (See Tip 14 in Chapter 3 for more information on manual mode.)

Select Panoramic Mode   If your camera has it, use panoramic mode. This mode allows you take a sequence of shots with a fixed exposure and often provides guides to help you overlap the shots correctly.

Transfer the Files to a Computer   You can use any number of software programs designed to combine your sequence of images into a single panorama. (See Chapter 8 for more information on moving images to your computer.) Adobe Photoshop Elements comes with a built-in stitching program call Photomerge, and it is amazingly easy to use.

Following are the basic steps involved in using Photomerge to produce a panorama:

1. Open the program, and you are prompted to add the sequence of files you downloaded from your camera. The default for the program is to attempt to stitch the photos automatically, which works pretty well if you've used one

of the tripod heads made for shooting stitched panoramas. If that's not the case, try unchecking the option Attempt To Automatically Arrange Source Images under Settings and then choose OK.

2. The Photomerge screen appears with thumbnails of your images in the upper window.

3. Choose the thumbnail of your first image and drag it into the lower window. Then do the same with the second image. You will notice that the second image becomes semitransparent as you move it over the first image (see Figure 7-2). This allows you to visually align similar features from both images.

4. Line up the two images as best you can and the program will do the rest. It seems like a bit of magic as they merge, but the program actually uses blending algorithms to stitch them together.

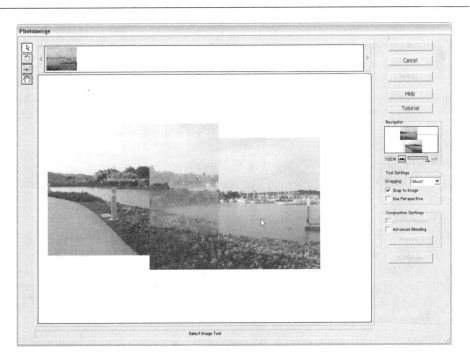

FIGURE 7-2   In Elements' Photomerge you can drag the thumbnails to the lower window and match up the edge details.

5. Repeat this process with as many images as you have in your sequence. When you are done, choose OK and the program will render the final panorama.

6. Now you can use the Photoshop Elements tools to crop, adjust color, and touch up the new panoramic image as necessary.

41. Shoot Movies

As you learned in Tip 20 in Chapter 3, switching your camera to video mode enables it to shoot short video clips that can be played back on your camera's preview, your computer's media player, or on the Web. You can even record them to tape or DVD and include them in your personal archive. If you only need short movies, then you may be able to save yourself the expense of a separate video camera. Try out your camera's movie-making abilities and see what you can do.

Why Would I Shoot a Movie?

As the old saying goes, "A picture may be worth a thousand words, but a movie has thousands of pictures." Because a movie captures a larger slice of time than a single frame is able to, it is particularly suited for recording something that is changing over time, such as the scoring moment in a sports event or a child's first steps. And although you may already own a video camera, you may find there are times when it isn't practical to carry it with you. The advantage of a digital camera is that by switching it from single-shot to video mode, you can still capture important events with motion and sound, producing a priceless record. (Try that with your conventional camera!) You can download those movie files into your computer, and then e-mail them to relatives and friends or publish them on your Web page.

Videos also can be a practical tool to use for business purposes. For instance, shooting a quick tour through a property can be helpful to a real estate agent and can show much more than static photos. The same files can be exported to a database, displayed on a business Web site, incorporated into a presentation, or transmitted via e-mail to other offices or directly to a client. Or you could record a demonstration of how to attach two components and post for viewing by service reps in the field. The ability to shoot short movies adds another dimension to your picture-taking experience, making your digital camera your portable multimedia production facility.

How Do I Set Up and Shoot a Movie with a Digital Camera?

The rules for shooting a movie with a digital camera are pretty much the same as for a standard video camera, only simpler. Following are some guidelines for setting up and shooting a proper movie.

Set Up the Shot   First, you need to know in advance what you want to shoot and make sure it will fit into the time duration limitations imposed by your camera. If the subject matter you want to shoot takes 2 minutes and your camera only can shoot video for 30 seconds, you are obviously not going to get it all. The video time duration limitations are listed in your camera's manual. The camera will also display a countdown meter to tell you how much shooting time you have left. The average maximum shooting time for a single movie sequence is about 30 seconds. If possible, do a quick run-through before you record the shot. This will help you avoid excessive reshoots.

Be aware of your lighting situation over the course of the entire shooting time. Your flash will not be operational when you are shooting a movie (it can't recycle fast enough), so you have to work with available light or have other external light sources. When you're shooting inside, you will need a fairly bright and consistent lighting source to get a good exposure. You can set up external floodlights to brighten the environment.

Finally, try to place yourself in a good position relative to what you want to shoot so you won't need to move during shooting.

Setting Up the Camera   Place the camera in video mode (see Tip 20, in Chapter 3); if your camera doesn't have video mode, you can use burst mode (see Tip 18, in Chapter 3). If you are using burst mode to capture a series of still pictures, you can download the individual frames and use a video-editing program to turn them into a movie. The movie won't have the smooth motion of a video, however, and will be more jerky, like a flip-card animation.

Shooting the Movie in Video Mode   Try to remain in a fixed position throughout the shot. Holding a digital camera steady while walking about is next to impossible, and you'll end up with something that looks like a *Blair Witch Project* effect (jumpy and rough). In addition, avoid rapid camera movements unless you want your audience to get queasy. The slower frame rates of MPEG movies also increase the negative effect of rapid movement by making the movie jerky. If you want to move the camera, pretend you are moving in slow motion or use a video-style tripod that allows for smooth panning and tilting.

Relating to movement, use your zoom feature sparingly. One of the most common errors the beginner makes in shooting movies is to zoom in and out constantly. If it is important to zoom, do it as slowly as you can and only do it once. All movement should be subtle.

If you are staging the movie, use a signal to begin and end action. When you are shooting for such a short duration, you don't want to waste valuable seconds.

Be sure to keep the action within the frame. Because LCD screens often refresh too slowly to show a movie sequence smoothly, it is best to use your camera's optical viewfinder. Also, be careful of bright backlighting created by windows or lamps, for example, which can throw off your exposure and silhouette your subject.

If you are recording sound, try to keep a constant distance from the sound source so you don't get big changes in the sound levels. If you want to say something while you are shooting, just realize that you are close to the microphone, so talk softly.

Finally, remember that you can erase any movie and shoot it over if you need to.

42. Shoot Animation for the Web

Animation covers a broad spectrum of style and technique. Everything from flip-page stick figures to Disney-style animated movies. One thing is for sure: digital techniques are becoming a common part of all animated works. This section covers animation as it relates to Web production.

We have all seen short animation pieces when we surf the Web. They often appear in banner ads and on portal pages. Web animation uses a special file format called GIF (Graphics Interchange Format) that allows a sequence of images to be played with definable parameters that control certain aspects of display. You can produce these animation files in a number of ways, and you can use any number of image sources. In this tip, I'll explain how shooting a sequence of movements can be converted into an animation that you can play on the Web.

Why Would I Want to Shoot a Web Animation?

Movement can be an irresistible attention-getter if it isn't so big or pervasive that it becomes annoying. Animations are eye-catching and can relate a lot of information in a short time. Adding animation to a Web site can bring new life to the media and guide the viewer's eye to points of particular interest. Animations also can be used to demonstrate something that is hard to convey with words or still pictures alone—such as the proper tennis swing or how to prune a tree. Such a process or gesture is best understood by seeing it in motion.

How Do I Use a Photographed Sequence to Produce Animation?

Burst and time-lapse mode sequences (see Tips 18 and 19 in Chapter 3) can provide a foundation for building many sorts of animation; just make sure that all the images are the same size and format. Animation files for the Web are usually in the form of GIF files. The GIF format allows a sequence of image files of the same size to be stacked up, so to speak, and played in succession, thus creating an animation. The individual images are most dramatic when they re-create a simple sequence of motion—such as someone walking, a ball bouncing, or a butterfly flapping its wings.

You can approach shooting for animation in a number of ways:

- You can use the object animation technique. You make small changes to the scene, photograph each change, and then put them together in an animation file, such as the series of clock hands in motion over an hour depicted in Figure 7-3. To execute this technique successfully, the camera must be fixed in one position—and it requires a lot of patience on your part. Claymation is another example of object animation technique; think of *Gumby*, the "Wallace and Gromit" movies, and the California Raisins ads.

- You can use a burst mode sequence for capturing a series of short-interval time slices of motion. This is good for depicting an average motion, such as walking—you can capture a model walking down the runway, for example. If you want really smooth motion from a burst mode series, have your subject move in slow motion so that there's not too much movement between shots.

FIGURE 7-3   A sequence of shots can be combined to produce an animation.

■ If you're more interested in a slideshow than a movie, you can use a series of images that don't have any inherent animated connection to create a slideshow effect. They could be a series of faces, travel shots, or artworks. Many of the programs that do GIF animation will let you time the duration of each frame in the sequence.

GIF animations are produced by specialized software applications, or in some cases, as a routine in your image editor. (See Tip 90 in Chapter 13 for more on using an image editor to create GIF animations.) A number of good programs let you create GIF animations from a sequence of photographic images. Ulead GIF Animator, Microsoft GIF Animator, GIF Construction Set, and Animagic, to name a few, will automate the process.

Part II

Digital Darkroom Magic

Chapter 8

Moving and Managing Your Pictures

So far I have focused on what you can do with your digital camera. Now I will shift the focus to that other wonderful invention, the computer. This chapter will concentrate on the process of moving images from your camera to the computer so you can begin the process of editing your photos in the digital darkroom. I will also present the best methods for managing your collection of digital photographs so you can store and catalog them correctly, giving you easy access anytime you need it. Learning good image-management techniques first will make your experience with editing photographs later more rewarding.

43. Transfer Images Directly from Camera to Computer

Now that you have filled up your camera's memory card with stunning pictures, you'll need to transfer those images to your computer to manage, edit, and print them. The process of moving the images to the computer is called *downloading*. It involves transferring the digital data stored on your memory card to the hard disk in your computer. The computer is your digital darkroom, image catalog, and print manager. Give the computer the digital "film" and you can take advantage of all the tools that your system provides.

Why Should I Download Images from Camera to Computer?

Because your camera is limited in the number of images it can store, you need to move them off the camera and onto a memory storage device. Memory cards can store a few images to more than a hundred, depending on the capacity of the card and resolution at which you are shooting. Memory cards are not cheap, so you wouldn't want to use them as permanent storage solutions. To keep reusing a memory card, you need to download the images from the card to another memory device, such as a handheld computer, a laptop, or a desktop computer, so you can erase the card and start shooting and storing again.

The computer is also the best way to manage your collection. You will be surprised at how fast you can build up a significant library of photos. The computer makes it a breeze to arrange your photos into albums, which makes finding a photo as quick and easy as a few mouse clicks—instead of having to rummage through old shoeboxes of snapshots.

After you load the images onto the computer, you can begin the real work of editing the images. Because the computer can display the full resolution of each shot, you can see and manipulate all the detail you captured.

Image-editing applications provide easy-to-use tools that help you enhance your digital images. With these tools, you can adjust color, size, and many other elements. In some applications, you can even produce templates for items you print on a regular basis, such as cards, calendars, newsletters, and scrapbook prints (see Chapter 14). You can also set up your printer to produce the best possible prints of your digital images.

What Is a Direct Transfer?

A *direct transfer* sends information back and forth between the camera and the computer through a direct cable connection. With this connection, the camera acts as the card reader so the memory card remains in the camera. You should familiarize yourself with your camera's options for output (see Figure 8-1). Older and low-end cameras commonly use a standard serial connection, which is slow. Newer and more expensive cameras often use faster connections such as universal serial bus (USB), Small Computer System Interface (SCSI), and FireWire. USB is quickly becoming the more accepted standard in consumer cameras, even though FireWire is much faster and favored by professionals.

Serial port

USB port

FIGURE 8-1   Typical output ports on the camera

Why Use the Direct Method?

The cable and software used to perform direct transfer are usually provided with the camera, and the receiving ports on the computer are typically standard equipment, so there is nothing extra to buy. You also get the flexibility of being able to connect to many different computers so long as they have a compatible port and the software is loaded, and you have to carry only a simple cable with you. With the new, high-speed connection standards like USB and FireWire, it can take just a few moments to download the contents of your camera to your computer. This is a far cry from the standard serial connections, which can take up to a half hour. USB connections can be made while the computer is still running and allow your computer to *sense* the camera when it is connected, bringing up the download software automatically in some cases.

Performing direct image transfer can drain the batteries on your camera quickly, so if you are performing transfers in the field, you will need to have extra batteries on hand. When you can, you should use a power adapter to avoid draining the batteries. The connections for USB and serial ports are often in the back of the computer, making them less convenient to connect. With the standard serial connection, you must shut down the computer before connecting and disconnecting or risk damage to your camera or computer.

How Do I Perform a Direct Transfer?

1. Load the software that came with your camera and follow the instructions in the install program (you need to do this the first time only).

2. Check your manual to determine what type of connection your camera supports and where the ports are located on your camera and computer (see Figure 8-1).

3. Locate the cable that came with your camera. If it is a standard serial cable, check with your vendor to see whether higher-speed options might be available.

4. Connect the cable to the port on your camera and then to the matching port on your computer. With a standard serial connection, make sure the computer and camera are turned off when you connect the cable or you risk damaging your equipment.

5. Plug in your power adapter if you are in a place where you can use one and you happen to have your power adapter with you.

6. If you are using a standard serial cable, power up your system and camera.

7. Run the software you loaded for your camera and download the images from your camera to a folder on your hard disk. Some cameras repeat the same file names for each download session; this means that if you download new images to the same folder where old images are stored, you will overwrite the older images. If your camera writes unique names for each session, you will avoid this problem. Double-check that all your pictures transferred properly before erasing the memory card.

8. If you need to download other memory cards, you can insert them into your camera and continue to download them in succession.

9. Power-down to disconnect a standard serial cable.

10. You can now erase or reformat the memory card(s) in the camera (check your manual for specific instructions) and you are ready to shoot again. Check your battery levels.

> **NOTE** *Although your camera's memory card looks to your computer just like a removable drive, it's usually a bad idea to erase or format image cards from the computer. The camera often uses special headers that include specific instructions for each file and these won't be included unless you let the camera format the drive.*

44. Use a Card Reader to Transfer Images to a Computer

A *card reader* is a small solid-state electronic device that lets you insert a memory card into a slot and read it as a disk drive on your computer screen (see Figure 8-2). It works in much the same way as the slot that reads the card in your camera. External card readers are small and portable, and unique card readers are available for each type of memory card. (See Tip 10 in Chapter 2 for more on memory cards.) Card readers either mount internally or they are attached to the computer through a parallel, serial, USB, SCSI, or FireWire cable connection. If your computer(s) have FireWire ports, get FireWire card readers. They will transfer a card full of files in seconds. In addition, SmartMedia adapters, which look like floppy disks, can be inserted into a standard 3.5-inch disk drive. Adapters are also available for PCMCIA slots, most commonly found on portable computers, that will accept SmartMedia and CompactFlash cards. If your card reader takes CompactFlash cards (the most popular format), make sure it takes Type II so that you can move up to the higher-capacity format as prices continue to fall.

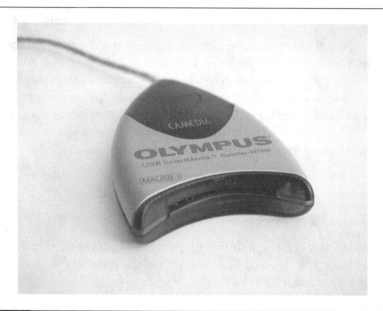

FIGURE 8-2   Typical card reader

NOTE

You can obtain multiple-format card readers that can read a number of card formats and offer the greatest amount of flexibility so that you can accept cards from other cameras and other devices.

Why Should I Use a Card Reader?

Card readers use less battery power by not using the internal card reader of the camera. You simply insert the memory card into the card reader to download the pictures, and the camera can be somewhere else entirely. This is ideal for business applications in which the camera needs to be out in the field while the office staff is downloading and managing images with the card reader. These memory cards are small and easily transferable. The card reader's interface looks like a regular disk drive. If you are familiar with working with a computer, you do not need to learn anything new. (Sigh of relief!)

How Do I Use a Card Reader?

Card readers are easy to use. Install some simple driver software, connect the card reader to your computer, insert the memory card, and you are ready to rock and roll.

An extra drive letter will appear in your computer's main directory. Explore the contents as you would on a normal drive. If you are using an adapter, insert the memory card into the adapter and then insert it in the appropriate PCMCIA slot or disk drive on the computer. The card must be inserted correctly or damage may occur.

45. Move Images from One Computer to Another

You may need to move images from one computer, such as a desktop, laptop, or handheld device, to another computer that may be as close as the next desk or as far away as Timbuktu. The ability to move around these images in so many ways is part of what makes digital imaging exciting.

Why Would I Move Images to Another Computer?

Digital images can be used in a variety of ways, and it is often useful to be able to share them with others. For example, your child may want to use one of your photos for a school project, or your boss may want to include a photo in a newsletter. Digital images are as portable as any other file on your system.

How Do I Move Images to Another Computer?

You can transfer digital images to other computers in a variety of ways.

Disk Transfer   The simplest solution is to use a standard 3.5-inch floppy disk that can be read by every computer. The drawback, however, is that a 3.5-inch disk offers only 1.4MB of space, so if you have photos of medium resolution, you will not be able to store too many images on a disk. With high-resolution photos, you may not even be able to store a single image.

A better approach is to equip your computer with a CD burner (a special CD drive that can use either write-once or rewriteable media). CDs can hold as much as 700MB of information, and blank write-once CDs are inexpensive, at just pennies apiece. Two types of blank, writeable CDs are available: CD recordable (CD-R) and CD rewritable (CD-RW). CD-Rs can be written to just once and cannot be erased (which makes them ideal for keeping permanent archives of original files), but CD-RWs can be erased and written to many times. Writing to CDs is quickly becoming popular due to easy-to-use software and the increased speeds of CD drives. With modern software such as Click 'n Burn or Roxio CD writing software, recording images is as simple as selecting and dragging the files into a window and then clicking the Record button.

Using a ZIP drive (from Iomega) makes sense if you are transferring large images or large quantities of smaller images. Several types of ZIP drives are available. Some offer 100MB of storage, while others offer up to 1GB. They are magnetic media, so they can be rewritten many times. Writing to them is also much quicker than writing to most CD recorders. The downside is that the disks cost approximately $10 to $12 apiece—about 30 times the price of a CD. Because ZIP drives are magnetic, they are not as reliable for long-term storage.

Network Transfer   A network is composed of hardware and software that link computers together. This link enables systems to communicate using a standard protocol. One good reason to use a network is to be able to transfer and share large amounts of data between systems efficiently. Systems connected to the network must have a network card and either a cable or wireless connection. You can move images to any shared space on other systems as easily as you can move an image to another folder on your own system.

Two things you must watch for when transferring images over a network. Be sure that you are using a high-speed (100 Mbps) connection—especially if you need to transfer several high-resolution files at a time. Also, if you need to transfer folders jam-packed with high-resolution files, even a small glitch in the signal is likely to freeze or abort the transfer. In that case, it's safer to write your libraries to a CD. Besides, you create an archival backup at the same time.

Internet Transfer   The Internet is a network that links computer systems globally. When you are online, you are actually linked to millions of other computers. This interconnected world gives you the ability to transfer your images to anyone who is connected to this worldwide network. As soon as you place an image on a Web page, it can be downloaded by anyone who views that page, no matter where they are. If you are looking for feedback on your work, the Internet is a good place to get exposure.

You can transfer images over the Internet in a number of ways:

- ■ **E-mail**   You can attach small JPEG files to e-mail messages (see Tip 89 in Chapter 13).

- ■ **Web pages**   Small JPEG images work well. If you want to download an image off the Web, you simply right-click the image and choose Save Image As. Be aware that images may be copyrighted, so you should read the terms of use.

- ■ **Message programs**   ICQ (I Seek You), AOL Instant Messenger, Yahoo! Messenger, IRC (Internet Relay Chat), and other programs provide options for transferring files to other systems.

■ **FTP**   Using File Transfer Protocol, you can transfer and receive files that are stored on a *server* (a computer system that acts as a host for Web sites and is directly tied to the Internet). You will need to check with your Internet Service Provider (ISP) to see whether it provides this kind of service. You can use programs such as WS-FTP, a file transfer program designed to access these sites. This is commonly used to transfer information to and from Web sites.

46. Sort Images by Category on the Computer

Sorting involves rearranging the images in a logical order. Think of it as an organized filing system. Digital images can be sorted visually, which is really the only way that makes sense.

What Are Categories?

The sorting categories can be anything you devise that helps you organize your images. Some typical categories could be family, friends, business, special events, and so on. You can also create subcategories to further refine your structure. If your category is flowers, for example, you might break it down further into types, such as roses or orchids.

Why Sort Images?

Sorting is a time-saving device. As you build your library of photos, you may realize that the file names fall short of providing enough information to help you easily locate the images. If time is valuable to you, you may find it necessary to develop a better strategy for managing all these images so you can access those that you need in an efficient manner. This entails a process of going through your collection and moving images into groups with common themes. Who has time to sift through hundreds, or thousands, of photos every time you want to find something?

How Do I Sort Images into Categories?

If your operating system allows you to view the images in folders as *thumbnails* (miniature images), you are a step ahead (see Figure 8-4 in Tip 47 in this chapter). If not, check the software that came with your camera. Most come with some sort of image-management software (see Tip 48 in this chapter). If the answer is no to both, you can buy one of many programs on the market to provide this capability.

FIGURE 8-3   Photoshop Elements file browser

Image editors are now getting better at image management, an example of which you can see in Figure 8-3. (Photoshop Elements 2 and Adobe Photoshop 7 ship with built-in image managers.) If you search the Web for *image management*, you'll find a host of available programs. There are even very capable shareware programs, such as ThumbsPlus and ACDsee, that you can simply download from the Web. Whatever image manager you choose, you should make sure it displays the image formats you use. It should also allow you to access the file system so you can sort, delete, copy, move, rotate, and rename your images. Being able to see a blown-up view of each image is another plus. Extra features that are also useful are the ability to perform simple image corrections and editing, make contact sheets, run slideshows, and perform batch operations (perform a task on many files at once).

After your images are displayed in thumbnail view, you can begin the process of categorizing them:

1. Navigate to where you want to store your images.

2. Create a new folder. Type a name for a category you want to store and then press ENTER.

3. Repeat step 2 for each category you want to create. If you want to create a subcategory, double-click a main category and then repeat step 2.

4. Navigate to where the pictures you need to sort reside.

5. View these pictures in thumbnail mode so you can easily identify them.

6. Open the originating folder and the folder that you want to move your files to so that they are side-by-side.

7. Drag the images to the appropriate category folder that you created.

If you don't like a folder system you created, try a file-naming scheme to categorize your files. This naming scheme makes it easy to find a file in any category, even if it has been misplaced. Simply name your files with a fixed prefix. For example, if you have a nature category, all files in this category could begin with *NAT*. After that prefix, you can add some descriptive text, such as *-Lake Mead*. So your complete file name will look like this: *NAT-Lake Mead.jpg*. When you need to find all image files within a given category, you could simply search for the category name.

47. Manage Images with Windows XP

Windows XP Home Edition is the newest beginner-level PC operating system from Microsoft. The Professional Version incorporates many of the features found in professional-level operating systems like Windows NT and 2000, but it's far more user friendly. Windows XP is much more stable and efficient than its predecessors—Windows 95, 98, and Me. It also provides many built-in tools for managing images. If you are serious about working with digital images on your PC, you should consider using XP.

Why Should I Use Windows XP to Manage Images?

The nice thing about image management in Windows XP is that it is built into the file system. Past versions of Windows required that you load third-party software to get the same features that come standard with Windows XP—one less thing to worry about if you're a digital photographer. Windows XP allows you view images as names, icons, thumbnails, filmstrips, or slideshows. Windows XP's system for dealing with digital images can save you time and frustration in managing a large collection. Windows XP also provides a great foundation for working with image-editing programs.

NOTE *When you are working within a graphics application, Windows XP allows you to view images in various modes from any Explorer window. Just click the Views menu, and then choose a view option from the pop-up menu.*

How Do I Use Windows XP to Manage Images?

Windows XP can help you view and manage digital images in a number of ways. You can view thumbnails within any folder by one of the following methods:

- Choose Views | Thumbnails.

- Choose Views icon | Thumbnails on the Standard Buttons Options bar and you will see the thumbnail views displayed in the folder window (see Figure 8-4).

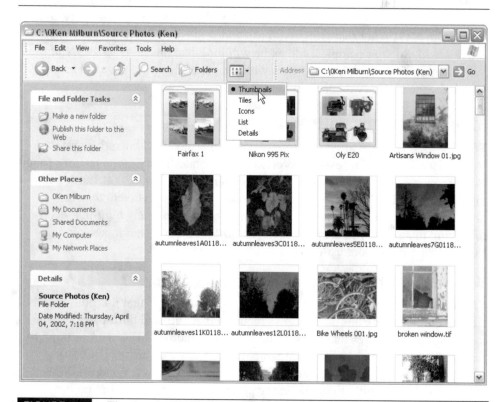

FIGURE 8-4   The thumbnail views in a Windows XP folder

You can perform any of the normal file operations on any thumbnail, such as copy, cut, rename, and delete, and you can drag the image to a new directory.

In thumbnail view, any subfolders with images inside will display four thumbnail samples of the images in that folder to help you identify the contents visually.

Here's how you can also enable any folder to view filmstrips:

1. Choose Views | Customize This Folder. The Properties window with the Customize tab will appear (see Figure 8-5).

2. Choose Photo Album from the pull-down menu under What Kind Of Folder Do You Want? This will activate the Filmstrip option on the Views menu.

3. The Filmstrip option allows you to scroll through a list of thumbnails at the bottom of the window and choose an image to display larger, as shown in Figure 8-6. You can also use the forward and back arrows to proceed one

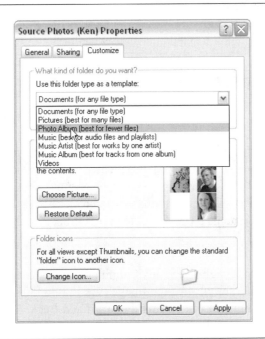

FIGURE 8-5   The folder Properties dialog box, where you can optimize the settings for photographs

The Filmstrip view

image at a time, and rotate the image with the rotate image buttons to the right of the arrows. This will permanently change the orientation of the image and will force resampling of your original JPEG file, which will cause some loss of image data. The file browser built into Photoshop 7 and Photoshop Elements 2.0 will rotate the thumbnail without resampling the original.

You can also double-right-click any thumbnail image to open the Picture and Fax Viewer to see a larger view of the image (see Figure 8-7). Along the bottom of the window are a number of controls: Forward and Back, Best Fit, Actual Size, Slide Show, Zoom, Rotate, Delete, Copy, and Print.

EXCITEMENT

The slow shutter speed that caused some blurring in the child's hands actually serves to show his wonder and excitement. Deep shade provided soft lighting and it only took three Quick Fix adjustments to make this a perfect shot.

COASTER CRUZ

The subtle colors illustrate the advantage of shooting in late afternoon on a winter's day. Color was manually rebalanced using the Photoshop Levels command. Shadow detail was lightened by painting in white on a transparent layer using the Soft Light command.

BOTTLED UP

Keep your eye out for the shapes and qualities of light that you may have overlooked on account of familiarity. It sometimes pays just to explore with the viewfinder glued to your eye. This shot was romanticized a bit by isolating the Diffuse Glow filter to the view out the window.

FRUIT STAND

This photo clearly demonstrates the advantage of using an extreme wide-angle add-on lens. Note that the image is in focus from the nearest orange to the farthest building, providing the viewer the feeling of being right in the scene.

WAITING

This photograph was made in late afternoon on a slightly hazy summer day. The feeling of Rembrandt-like classical lighting was created with a Photoshop Elements built-in artistic effects filter, called Dry Brush, applied to a duplicated layer. The "dry-brushed" layer was then made partially transparent and partially erased so that details of the original photograph could be seen through it. Finally, the Burn and Dodge tools were used to emphasize certain areas of the photo.

NEWS TODAY

Careful choice of a wide-angle zoom and kneeling to get a low point-of-view made for the strong composition in this picture of a couple reading the Sunday paper. Photoshop Elements 2.0 was used to progressively blur the background to reduce apparent depth-of-field.

SUNSET HARBOR

Sunrise and sunset are two of the best times to take pictures. The lighting is dramatic and rich in color, yet shadows are open enough to show detail, and skies tend toward the dramatic.

STAIRWAY TO JAPAN

This image was taken with a supplementary wide-angle lens, which greatly contributes to the feeling of depth. Two exposures were combined into one by sandwiching them onto separate layers with the lightest layer on top. I then erased through the top layer to reveal those areas that needed to be darker.

MAGNOLIAS

Notice how much influence the play of light and the arrangement of existing objects can strengthen a composition. Part of the trick in making this work lay in taking pictures from several points-of-view. Remember, digital pictures are free—once you pay for the camera.

SERIOUS BABY

This was one of those moments I couldn't resist preserving. Three Photoshop Elements Quick Fix adjustments corrected the color, contrast, and exposure, and the Clone tool removed some stray elements.

FUN ON WHEELS

Sometimes the feeling of action is best captured with a slow shutter speed. This photo of a cycling couple was shot at 1/40 of a second while panning the camera to keep the girl's head in the same position, thus blurring the background.

LIZ

Here is a photo of my friend Liz taken in a sunlit pasture. Fill light from the camera's built-in flash keep the shadows from being too harsh. The background was softened to decrease depth-of-field.

ICE JUNGLE

A supplementary telephoto lens coupled with having the Nikon mounted on a tripod did most of the work to create this highly textured photo of ice plant and tropical foliage. The Photoshop Elements Auto Contrast command and a wee boost in color saturation did the rest.

PERFORMERS

Because digital cameras are small, you can keep them with you at all times.
I shot this when magician/contortionist/juggler/comedian Frank Olivier, his
wife, and their brand-new baby stopped at my car to say hello. You just
never know when the next generation of performers will come along.

PURPLE PASSION

Flora and fauna never cease to be fascinating and beautiful. Keep your eye on the garden and you're almost sure to produce some lovely pictures. I set a Nikon CP5000 camera in automatic exposure mode using the spot meter settings to ensure sharp focus on the pistils of the flower.

CAT'S EYE VIEW

It pays to get close to your subject, or to do anything else that gives you a fresh and unusual point-of-view. This picture was taken with a Nikon 995 camera, which can take very close-up pictures without a supplementary lens.

FIGURE 8-7   The Windows Picture and Fax Viewer

48. Use Your Camera's Image Catalog Software

Most camera manufacturers provide image catalog software that lets you control the download of your images from your camera, view your images as thumbnails, reorganize them to folders, rotate them, perform standard file operations, and in some cases perform basic image correction and image editing.

Why Would I Use Image Catalog Software?

If your operating system does not support thumbnail views and image management, you can use the software features offered by the camera manufacturer at no extra cost. This software also supports the direct download features of your camera, so you will need it if you are planning to use that method.

How Do I Use Image Catalog Software?

Image catalog software acts as an interface when the camera connects directly to the computer for downloading images. The software often has the added bonus of providing image-management abilities after you get the images off of the camera and onto the computer. Figure 8-8 shows such an interface for the Olympus Camedia.

Most of these programs operate in a number of modes. The exact functions will vary among manufacturers and from one camera model to another. The

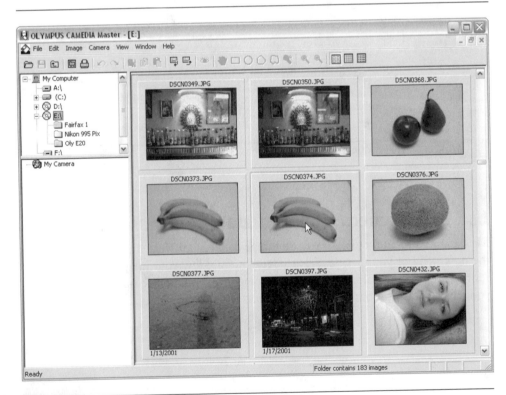

FIGURE 8-8   The Olympus Camedia Master interface

following discussion covers the general mode functions typically found in this type of software, but you'll need to consult your camera's user guide for more information.

Camera Mode   In this mode, the program is operating the camera remotely from your computer through the direct connection. You can download the images stored on the camera memory card, change settings in the camera, and reorganize and erase images on the memory card. Moreover, it is the camera, not the computer, that does the erasing.

Image Mode   This mode provides a full thumbnail view of all the images you have downloaded and lets you manipulate them in a variety of ways. This may take the form of file commands, image-editing commands, or batch-processing commands. File commands let you perform standard File menu functions such as move, copy, cut, paste, delete, rename, and so on. Image-editing commands let you resize, crop, change color and value settings, rotate, apply filters, and so on. Batch processing allows you to perform file or editing commands on a group of files at one time.

Another useful feature in most of the newer software is somewhat hidden, but valuable. It has to do with a new file format called EXIF (Exchangeable Image File Format) JPEG or EXIF TIF. This file format allows the camera to record all the pertinent information about each shot and place it in the image file itself. This information can be retrieved later by any program that knows how to read the file correctly. This format is catching on fast and provides a permanent record of the settings you used on each shot so you can avoid what went wrong and duplicate what went right. Figure 8-9 shows image file information provided by EXIF JPEG.

49. Rotate Images

Most of the modern software that helps you to manage images (such as Windows XP, Mac OS X, the new versions of Photoshop, and the software that comes with most any $200-and-up digital camera) provides you with the means to easily rotate thumbnails.

Why Would I Rotate an Image?

As you will quickly learn, rotating the camera 90 degrees is something you do about half the time, in order to more precisely frame subjects that are vertical in nature, such as people and doorways. This doesn't affect the image quality, but when you download the images, you will see that those images are rotated sideways—which makes it difficult to judge the subject's expression and the quality of the image's composition.

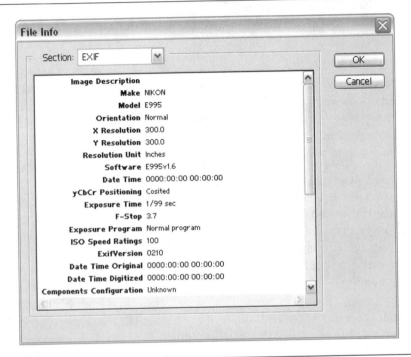

FIGURE 8-9   EXIF JPEG image file information

How Do I Rotate an Image?

The location of the Rotate command varies from one image-editing software program to another, so it is impossible to give you exact instructions. The majority of programs let you rotate an image 90 degrees clockwise or counterclockwise by clicking a button with an icon of a curved arrow that points in one of those two directions. In some programs, the command can be found on an Image menu, and in others you'll be able to right-click an image and choose the Rotate command from a context menu. Some programs, such as those in the Photoshop family, let you do it in all of the above ways. Look at the orientation of the image and decide whether you need to rotate the image clockwise or counterclockwise to get it back to the correct position. If the image is completely upside down, you can use 180-degree rotation to correct it—or just click one of the 90-degree rotation buttons twice.

Figure 8-10 shows the rotation values for an image.

Clockwise 90   Counterclockwise 90

180

FIGURE 8-10   File rotations

50. Archive Images to CD-R and CD-RW

As mentioned earlier in this chapter, CD-R (CD recordable) is a blank CD that, once written to with a CD burner (a special drive that can record data to CDs), cannot be erased or overwritten. It then becomes what is called read-only CD, because the data on the disk cannot be altered. The CD-RW (CD rewritable) can be written to, erased, and then written to again; it's reusable. CD-RWs are slightly more expensive than the CD-R discs, so if you don't plan to reuse your discs, save yourself the money. Another issue with CD-RW discs is they are not as compatible with other CD drives, which makes CD-R a better bet if you are transferring images to other computers or want to put photos on an affordable medium that can be passed on to friends or clients. You can even put a whole portfolio or scrapbook of images on one of the business card–sized CDs, which can be burned on any standard CD burner.

Why Should I Archive My Photos to CD?

Contrary to what a computer or camera salesperson may tell you, computer systems do have occasional problems, and you can lose information. Backing up important information is always a good idea. If keeping digital versions of your photographs is important, you need to consider a method for storing them safely.

Another consideration of archiving is the amount of space that digital images can consume on your system. Unless your system has large amounts of disk space available, your digital photographs can quickly fill up your hard disk.

CDs are one of the best ways to archive your photographs for a number of reasons:

- The discs are inexpensive—less than 50 cents apiece if you buy in bulk.

- They offer up to 700MB of storage space.

- The discs cannot be accidently erased like magnetic media, so your data is more secure.

- CDs enjoy universal support, so you can transfer information easily to others, regardless of what computer platform they use.

- New software for creating CDs is easy to use and reliable. It is also included with most all new computers that come with a CD burner built-in.

How Do I Save Images onto a CD?

You'll need to purchase a CD burner. The average price these days is $75–$150. If you're buying a new computer, you're almost certain to get a CD burner with it. The CD burner usually includes software that manages the process of writing to the CD. Not all CD burner software is created equal, and it's important that you get a good one to get reliable performance.

You'll also need blank CDs. You can pick them up at any computer supply store or on the Internet. You get the best price per disc if you buy in bulk—usually 25–100 CDs per pack.

Read the instructions that come with the CD burner to download your images to the disc.

51. Create Wallpaper from Your Images

Wallpaper is a single image or tiled images that covers the desktop of your computer screen and acts as a visual backdrop. This is strictly a decorative feature and has no real functionality other than being a pleasing diversion from looking at a blank screen.

Why Should I Use My Photos to Create Wallpaper?

If you like the photographs you take and would enjoy the opportunity to gaze into the lovely scene you photographed on that last vacation, making your own wallpaper gives you the chance to personalize your computer environment and put some of your photography on display. Photographs make a particularly good choice for wallpaper because they visually break the flat plane of the screen and can have the effect of looking out a window—which can be a relaxing experience not only for your brain but for your eyes as well.

How Do I Create Wallpaper?

Creating wallpaper for your Windows XP desktop is an easy process:

1. Position your cursor anywhere in the desktop, except on an icon, and then right-click the mouse button. From the pop-up menu, choose Properties to open the Display Properties dialog box.

2. Choose the Desktop tab, shown in Figure 8-11.

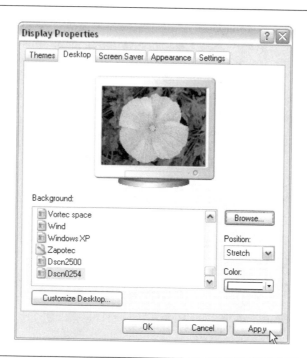

FIGURE 8-11 The Desktop tab in the Display Properties window

3. Click the Browse button. The Browse dialog box displays the My Pictures directory by default. Locate the image file you want to use as the new wallpaper, and then double-click it.

4. Select the appropriate option in the Position pull-down list to obtain the desired look.

5. Click the Apply button.

Try This: **Make a Desktop Slideshow, Using Windows XP or Photoshop Elements**

If you are running Windows XP, you can make a slideshow of your images. Gather all the photos you want to display into one folder. Choose Display Properties | Screen Saver, and then select My Pictures Slideshow from the Screen Saver drop-down menu. Click the Settings button to set the parameters for your slideshow.

Photoshop Elements will automatically make a slideshow that is a universally readable PDF file. You can attach the slideshow to an e-mail, put it on a Web page, or ship it to anybody on a CD. Then, with the Acrobat Reader installed (it's a free download from http://www.adobe.com/products/acrobat/), you just double-click the PDF icon and the slideshow starts playing—complete with transitions, such as wipes and dissolves between slides. Many other inexpensive image editors can create these slideshows as well.

Chapter 9

Correcting Images
with the Computer

We would all like to get a shot right the first time. It would be nice to take the perfect picture whenever we pressed the shutter button. No one can do that, though, so relax and learn how to work with image-editing tools to increase your success ratio. Any photographer will tell you that the darkroom is where half the battle is waged. If you can get a decent shot with your digital camera, chances are you will be able to make it into something better in the digital darkroom. For the purpose of demonstrating image-editing methods, I will be using Adobe's Photoshop Elements program throughout this book.

52. Rotate an Image to Correct Alignment

One of the Rotate command's useful features is its ability to correct misalignments of the image, which is most apparent when you take shots of subjects with straight edges, like buildings or a clear horizon line. Sometimes you can tilt the camera as you're shooting, so the objects in the shot are not lined up correctly with the edges of the frame.

It's also common for photos to be aligned incorrectly after they are scanned, because it's difficult to get them positioned perfectly straight on the scanner bed. The Straighten Image command makes this a breeze to correct.

Why Is Altering the Image in This Way Important?

When images are out of alignment, the viewer's attention is drawn away from the important parts of the photo and the composition is disrupted. The eye of the viewer wants to settle in with the photograph, not wrestle with trying to correct it. A misalignment will be the first thing that a viewer notices, no matter how good the photo is. The viewer's first impression will be that it is incorrect.

How Do I Use the Image-Editing Software to Correct This Problem?

Following are a few commands available in the Photoshop Elements program that can help you correct your images.

To realign a photo with the Rotate command, do this:

1. Open the image you want to realign in Photoshop Elements.

2. Choose Image | Rotate | Custom to open a dialog box in which you can enter the degrees of rotation, down to fractions of a degree, as necessary.

3. Enter the amount in degrees. You might find it helpful to start with a small number like 1 or .5 to get a sense of what works best. This is a trial-and-error method, but it usually takes only a few tries to get it right. Then choose whether you want to rotate left or right.

You can also adjust the alignment with Free Rotate, which allows you to rotate the picture by hand and align it by eye.

1. Choose Image | Rotate | Free Rotate Layer. When the transformation box appears over the image, place your cursor just to the outside of any corner handle until you see the Rotate icon appear. This icon looks like a curved, double-headed arrow.

2. Click and hold down the left mouse button and drag to rotate the image in any direction. Release the mouse button to set the new position.

3. The image will now be tilted and the corners will be outside the canvas. Unless you like this (um, ugly) effect, you'll want to trim the image so that the borders are upright and perfectly rectangular. You'll do this by cropping, which I'll show you how to do in the next tip in this chapter.

NOTE   *If you open a JPG image in your image editor, make certain that you save it as a TIF file to prevent losing additional picture information.*

To realign a photo that was scanned crooked, use the Straighten Image command:

■ Choose Image | Rotate | Straighten Image And Crop. The program will look at the angled edges of the image, adjust them to be parallel to the canvas, and then crop the image.

Figure 9-1 shows an image being rotated, and an image corrected and cropped.

53. Frame Your Shot with Cropping

Cropping is a method of cutting away portions of the image from any edge. Think of it as an electronic paper cutter or reframer. If, for example, you were standing too far back when you took the picture and captured detail that you really hadn't intended in the periphery, you can crop the shot to include just the subject you want in the frame. You may also want to crop an image that you've rotated, so that it will be straight again.

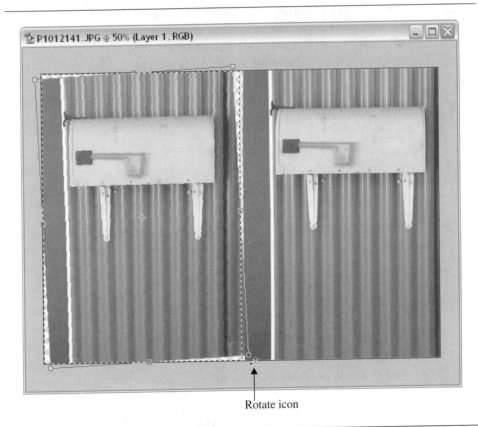

Rotate icon

FIGURE 9-1   The image on the left is being rotated to correct alignment; the image on the right has been corrected and cropped.

Why Do I Need to Crop My Image?

Even with your best efforts, you may end up with extra subject matter that doesn't complement your composition. (The importance of good composition and framing your photos properly is discussed in Chapter 4.) The Crop tool and Crop command provide you with an electronic cutting board to snip off unwanted portions of the image and thereby improve the composition, giving you another opportunity to reframe your shot after the image has been taken.

How Do I Crop an Image?

Here's how to crop an image using the Crop command:

1. Open the image you want to crop in Photoshop Elements.

2. Choose the Rectangular Marquee tool from the Toolbox, and drag it to define the area of the image you want preserve after the crop.

3. Choose Image | Crop. The portions of the image beyond the crop border are cut away.

Here's how to crop an image using the Crop tool:

1. Choose the Crop tool from the Toolbox.

2. Clear the Crop options by clicking the Clear button on the Options bar.

3. Drag the Crop tool to outline the area of the image you want to preserve. The area outside the box is shaded so you can visualize the crop more clearly, as shown in Figure 9-2.

4. Click the Commit icon on the Options bar, or double-click inside the crop area to finalize the crop.

flowers in window.tif @ 33.3% (RGB)

FIGURE 9-2   Cropping an image at left, and the final image at right

54. Use Quick Fix

The Quick Fix command is found in the Enhance menu of Photoshop Elements. Quick Fix is a virtual smorgasbord of tools you can use for correcting your photos. Quick Fix gathers basic and automated editing tools and presents them in a user-friendly way (see Figure 9-3). These tools include Auto Contrast, Auto Levels, Brightness/Contrast, Fill Flash, Adjust Back Lighting, Auto Color, Hue/Saturation, Auto Focus, Blur, Rotate 90 And 180 Degrees, and Flip.

Why Should I Use Quick Fix?

Quick Fix is a convenience. You don't have to use it because all the commands are also listed separately on the Enhance menu. However, Quick Fix provides easy access to the most common tools, a before-and-after comparison thumbnail, and tips on how to use each command. This makes it faster and easier to do those things that are most likely to bring the image up to a quality point where you are

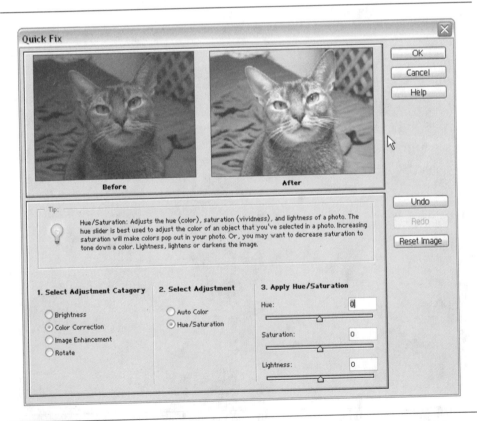

FIGURE 9-3   The Quick Fix interface

proud to show it to a friend or customer. That's important if you want to show off a few dozen pictures from an event or assignment in a hurry. It also offers a way to help maintain the quality of the image because the changes you make in the dialog are cumulative in their effect on the image, and that cumulative final effect is only used to change the image once, when you click OK, rather than once for each change you make. Finally, Quick Fix's ability to instantly preview the effect of any of its adjustments makes it a great learning tool that familiarizes you with editing features and the results they can produce. Of course, if you want a greater degree of control than the automated features can offer, you can always use the other commands available on the Enhance menu in addition to Quick Fix.

How Do I Use Quick Fix to Correct Images?

The Photoshop Elements' Quick Fix interface is easy to use. Here's how to perform a Quick Fix on an image:

1. Open an image you want to edit in Photoshop Elements.

2. Choose Enhance | Quick Fix. The Quick Fix dialog box will appear.

3. You will see the image previewed in two windows at the top of the dialog box, labeled *Before* and *After*. They will appear identical when you first open Quick Fix because you haven't performed any changes yet. The After image will change to reflect your changes as you make them.

4. The commands are broken down into four categories: Brightness, Color Correction, Image Enhancement, and Rotate in column 1, Select Adjustment Category. Choose one of the categories to adjust your image.

5. You will notice that the items change under column 2, Select Adjustment. Each major category in the first column has a set of adjustments associated with it that appear in the second column. The commands are grouped for a particular kind of edit, such as color correction, to make your job easier.

6. Choose an adjustment and you will see the controls for that adjustment appear in the third column. (In Figure 9-3, you can see how the information appears in all three columns.) If this is an automated adjustment, Quick Fix will ask you to apply it. All other adjustments will provide a series of sliders to alter the effects.

NOTE   *You can undo any adjustment by clicking the Undo button, or you can reset all the adjustments you have made in the current session by clicking the Reset Image button.*

7. When you are satisfied with your corrections, click OK to finalize them.

55. Alter the Color Balance

You can alter the color balance and create a mood using the Photoshop Elements Hue/Saturation command.

Correcting color balance is the proper tuning of color in an image to match our perception of how it *should* look. Color balance can be used to make photos look more natural or to enhance ambiance and mood by changing the effect of color on lighting. The colors are balanced when the overall relationship and perceived quality of the colors in the image are optimized for the look you want. Color balance also refers to the editing system of changing the colors in an image to be more optimized.

Why Do I Need to Adjust Color Balance?

We all know how environmental lighting in a restaurant or theatrical lighting at a live performance can affect our reactions and emotions. The same is true in color-adjusting a photograph. Lighting plays a significant role in how the mood in an image is set. The muted colors of a foggy day, the bright harsh colors of summer, or the soft glow of a sunset can help set the mood.

Because the camera cannot always capture the color as you envision it, it often becomes necessary for you to manipulate the existing color to achieve an effect. If the photograph is washed out, for example, you can bring up the color saturation to intensify the color and breathe new life into it. Shift the color hue, or perceived color, toward a cooler blue in a winter shot or add a touch more red to a photo of autumn leaves. This allows an ordinary photograph to produce more impact on our visual senses and emotions.

How Can Color Balance Tools Alter a Mood?

The Hue/Saturation command is used to adjust the color balance of an image. You might want to experiment a bit with the controls of this command to get used to how they affect the image. Keep your preview on so you can visually follow the effect of the changes you make. That will be your guide. This is about getting the photograph to match your vision, not just what you actually captured.

How Do I Use Color Balance?

Here's how to balance color with Hue/Saturation:

1. Open the image you want to color-balance in Photoshop Elements.

2. Choose Enhance | Adjust Color | Hue/Saturation. The Hue/Saturation dialog box, shown next, offers three slide controls:

- ■ **Hue**   Shifts the color in the entire image or selected region.

- ■ **Saturation**   Increases or decreases the intensity of the color. When the slider is shifted all the way to the left, all colors become gray. When the slider is shifted all the way to the right, the colors display their richest hue. Adjusting the saturation can add vibrancy to washed-out photos or surrealistic color to normal photos.

- ■ **Lightness**   Increases or decreases the brightness without changing hue or saturation.

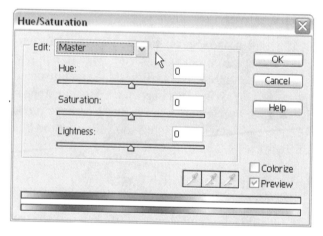

3. Choose a color range to work with from the drop-down menu at the top of the dialog box. Here, you can change all the colors in the image at once by choosing Master (the default), or you can choose preset ranges.

4. For a finer level of control, you can work with individual color ranges. You can choose individual color ranges from the drop-down menu.

5. You can also set up your own ranges using the eyedropper tools near the bottom of the dialog box to select colors from your image as a starting point, and then add or subtract colors with the + or − eyedroppers. Range sliders will appear over the color bars at the bottom of the dialog box, which can be moved to expand or contract the range. Ranges give you power to balance specific areas of color individually.

6. Another option is to choose the Colorize check box to convert the image to a color monotone, which gives you the effect of a tinted black-and-white photo. You can change the color of the tint by moving the Hue slider.

Try This: **Reverse Time with Tinting**

Use the Colorize option with a dark brown tint to achieve a good foundation for an antique photo look. Add some texture and a few torn edges and scratches to transpose a new photo into an "old" one. (Also see Tip 59, later in this chapter.)

---

56. Eliminate Color Cast

In Chapter 3, Tip 12, you learned about setting the white balance to help your camera accurately interpret the colors in the scene. Although this works most of the time, sometimes unusual lighting will still produce an unwanted shift in color. This shift is called *color cast*. When this happens, a shot can appear as though a colored light was cast over everything in the photo. You have probably seen a photo affected by color cast, in which it looks too yellow or too blue, and the people look really awful.

Why Do I Need to Eliminate Color Cast?

Although altering color cast can improve a photo, it can just as well make everything look unnatural and even downright unattractive. If changing the camera's white balance settings doesn't correct the problem, you can get a second chance at correcting color cast with image-editing software.

NOTE *You can see color cast if you are looking through the LCD. If you are unsure of the light, check the LCD for color exposure. Take a few test shots to see if different white balance settings can correct the problem.*

How Do I Eliminate Color Cast with Software Tools?

Photoshop Elements includes a handy tool called Color Cast, which makes dealing with color shifts as simple as a click of the mouse, provided you can find parts of your image that should be neutral (colorless). If there are no pure whites, grays, or blacks, you'll at least get some bizarre color cast effects. Here is how you do it:

1. Open the image in Photoshop Elements.

2. Choose Enhance | Adjust Color | Color Cast. The Color Cast dialog box appears.

Try This: **Click and Color**

When using the Color Cast command, click the eyedropper on other colors in the image and watch what happens. You can get some interesting color effects this way.

3. Use the eyedropper tool in the lower-right corner to select a color in the image that would appear to be black, white, or gray if the colors were not shifted. This is akin to setting the white balance.

4. Check the preview to see the color change immediately as you select the color. If the result is not to your liking, simply try again. Sometimes a stray pixel of an odd color can affect the outcome. When the color balance looks pleasing to you, stop.

NOTE
In portrait shots, if you can't find a good place to take an eyedropper reading, you can always use the whites of the eyes as a reference. White business shirts and black shoes or belts are also good references.

57. Get a Visual Fix on Corrections with the Color Variations Command

Color Variations is a system for adjusting color, saturation, and brightness using an addition and subtraction process. Thumbnail references enable you to see the relationship of the changes as they happen.

Why Should I Use This Command to Correct Images?

The Photoshop Elements Color Variations command provides an intuitive process for color correction that is ideal for beginners. This easy-to-use interface lets you see immediately how adding or subtracting color affects the image. You can also see how a number of changes alter the original image with before and after thumbnails. This makes the process totally visual, so you don't have to deal with separate processes that might be more difficult for the beginner to understand and integrate. The Color Variations command allows you to experiment with different combinations, and you can reset it as many times as you like before you finalize the changes. Just remember that the effect of each change is cumulative. That is, each change is made as an addition to any previous changes you made. Furthermore, the sum of these changes stays in effect until you click the Reset button to deliberately return all the settings to their defaults.

How Do I Use the Color Variations Command?

Here's how to apply color variations to an image using Photoshop Elements:

1. Open the image in Photoshop Elements.

2. Choose Image | Adjust Color | Color Variations. The Color Variations dialog box will appear, as shown in Figure 9-4.

3. Select an area to adjust under item 1. Midtones, Shadows, and Highlights limit the color changes to those general ranges with some overlap. The Saturation option adjusts the intensity of color for the whole image.

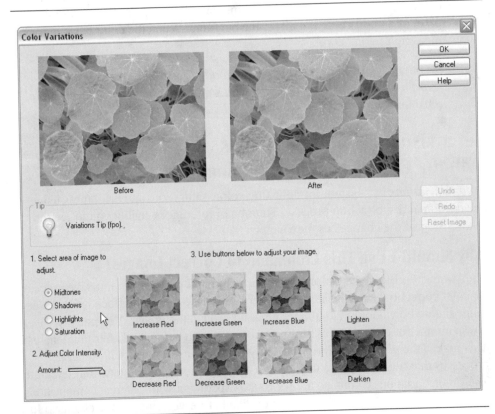

FIGURE 9-4   The Color Variations dialog box

4. Adjust the color intensity slider in item 2. This controls the amount of color correction that occurs when you click on one of the thumbnails. You can make subtle changes by moving the slider to the left and very obvious changes by moving the slider to the right.

5. In item 3, add and subtract color by clicking the thumbnails for each attribute, and observe the changes in the After box at the top of the dialog box. You can reset the image at any time and start again.

58. Create a Perfectly Exposed Image

Simply stated, *exposure* is the amount of light that is used to expose the image on the light-sensitive chips in the camera. The shutter speed and aperture setting control the exposure of light (see Chapter 3).

Why Do I Need to Get the Best Exposure?

The exposure of the image determines the quality of detail that can be properly rendered by the camera. If the image is overexposed (too much light), the details will be washed out. If it is underexposed (too little light), the highlights look dim and shadow detail drops out. A perfectly exposed image shows crisp highlights and good detail in the shadows, with a good contrast range throughout the image.

Perfect exposure is sometimes hard to achieve when taking pictures. The camera cannot always compensate for every lighting situation, and sometimes you need to go to the digital darkroom to correct the image.

NOTE   *An underexposed digital image is easier to work with than an overexposed image. Details can hide in dark areas of an image and be brought out by image-editing techniques, but once details are washed out by overexposure, much of them will be impossible to restore.*

How Do I Use Image-Editing Software to Optimize Exposure?

The Photoshop Elements Levels command is an advanced tool that offers a higher degree of control in adjusting your image than the Quick Fix and Color Variations commands.

Here's how to use the Levels command for correcting exposure:

1. Open the image in Photoshop Elements.

2. Choose Image | Enhance | Adjust Color/Brightness | Levels. You will see the Levels dialog box shown in Figure 9-5.

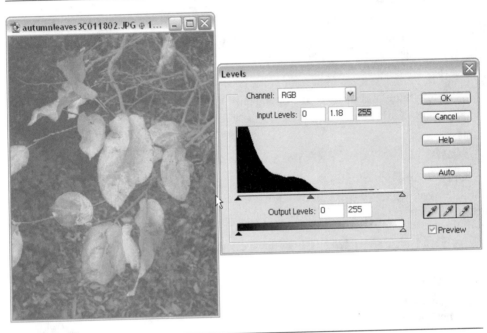

FIGURE 9-5   The Levels dialog box

3. The graph in the dialog box shows the distribution of pixels in the full tonal range from black (extreme left) to white (extreme right). The example in Figure 9-5 shows a dark, underexposed photo, in which most of the pixels are weighted to the dark side of the graph. If it were overexposed, the pixels would be weighted to the right side. This means that the vast majority of the pixels in this image are dark, and not much detail is available in the upper range. The leaves would be fairly bright if the image were properly exposed. The Levels command gives you ultimate control in correcting this. You want to shift some detail into a brighter range to increase the image range and contrast.

4. First, you should balance the exposure for each primary color: Press COMMAND-1 (Mac) or CTRL-1, or choose Red from the Channel menu at the top of the histogram. Then perform steps 5 and 6 that follow. Next, press COMMAND-2 (Mac) or CTRL-2, or choose Green from the Channel menu, and then do steps 5 and 6 again for that channel. Finally, press COMMAND-3 (Mac) or CTRL-3, or choose the Blue channel and repeat steps 5 and 6 one more time.

5. Slide the white triangle to the left until it is at the point where the graph starts to curve up (in this case, about halfway through the graph—see Figure 9-6). This is where the magic of levels takes place. When you change the slider, the program takes the newly defined graph segment (between the black and white arrows) and spreads it to cover the complete tonal range from black to white. This is shown in Figure 9-6. The image now has the maximum amount of value range to display detail properly.

6. Adjust the black triangle on the graph slider so that it just touches the histogram where it starts to rise.

7. Once you've expanded the brightness range to cover the entire histogram for each primary color, your image will have near-perfect color balance. Now, only now, and not one second before now, you can adjust your exposure. You should do that to all three channels equally in order to maintain color balance. So now and only now you will use the middle slider.

FIGURE 9-6   Adjusting the tonal range with the Levels command

First, choose the RGB (composite) channel from the Channel menu. Now, drag the gray (midtone) slider back and forth until you are happy with the overall brightness of the image. Your image is now color balanced and contains a pure white highlight, a solid black deep shadow, and perfect midtones. It's the digital version of Ansel Adams' famous Zone System.

NOTE *If the histogram is taller than the level part of the graph at either the white or black end, do not move that slider yet ... and probably never.*

59. Create Instant Effects

Photoshop Elements provides an Effects Palette that automates the process of applying special effects to your images, enabling preset routines that perform a series of operations on a selection, text, or a whole layer to produce unique effects.

Why Should I Use Instant Effects?

Would you want to eat bland food every day, or would you rather add some spices to enhance the flavor so the experience is richer? Instant Effects can add some visual spice to your digital-imaging projects. Digital imaging is exciting because you can go beyond the realms of pure photography and explore a broader range of visual beauty and art than you can with a camera alone. The "why" of using these effects comes from your personal need to express a larger view than snapshots alone can communicate. These effects let you be adventurous. On the other hand, overusing effects and using them "just for the sake of it" usually produces tragically trite results.

How Do I Use Instant Effects to Alter the Image?

Applying effects to your images is easy in Photoshop Elements.

1. Open an image in Photoshop Elements.

2. From the Window menu, choose Effects. The default menu will display, showing each of the effects in a thumbnail view so you can get a sense of what each effect does. Effect types are broken down into four categories:

   ■ **Text Effects**   Apply only to a text layer

   ■ **Image Effects**   Affect the whole image

- ■ **Textures**   Add a new layer with the texture applied

- ■ **Frames**   Alter the edges of the image

3. To apply an effect, click and hold down the left mouse button on the effect thumbnail; or, if you are working in List view, click and hold down the mouse on the effect name. The cursor will change to a grabbing hand.

4. Drag the effect over the image and release the mouse button. You can also select the effect and then click the Apply button at the upper-right of the palette. But wait! You can also apply the effect by double-clicking its icon in the Effects Palette.

60. Use Recipes for 31 Complex Solutions

In Photoshop Elements, recipes are lists of preset step-by-step instructions that perform a variety of tasks. They are an adjunct to the help system conveniently placed in an easy-to-access palette. These recipes are found in the How To Palette in the Palette well (at the right end of the Options bar).

Why Should I Use Recipes as Solutions?

Recipes are an excellent learning tool because they take you through common editing tasks one step at a time, like a good cookbook steps you through a recipe. The recipe tells you what tools you need and how to apply them properly. They also provide links in the text that automatically bring up the tools and commands that you need as you follow the procedures. Recipes are handy reference guides and valuable aids for the new user.

As Adobe releases more recipes, you can download them from the link provided in the drop-down menu on the How To Palette.

Try This: Shuffle the Deck and Get New Effects

Try experimenting with the effects to see how they alter your image. Stack different effects on separate layers and adjust the layer opacity factor, blend modes (see Chapter 12), or layer orientation to see how combined effects change your image.

How Do I Use Recipes to Achieve Solutions?

1. From the Window menu, choose How To. The Recipes Palette will appear.

2. From the Recipes menu, choose a category to access a list of recipes in a given category.

3. Choose a recipe, and then follow the step-by-step instructions in the wizard-type dialog that appears. Often, when the instructions might be a bit complicated, you're just told to click a button. Doing so performs several operations that will lead to accomplishing the effect you're after.

61. Draw Details Out of the Shadows and Highlights

When you take photographs in intense light, such as broad daylight, it is common for any dark shadows in the shot to hide some of the detail. Sometimes you can fill the shadows with the internal flash. The internal flash, however, does not deal with shadows that are farther away than the range of the flash—in some cases, they illuminate only up to 15 feet. If you end up with shadows that are too deep and hide detail, you can use the Fill Flash command in Photoshop Elements to help correct them. The beauty of this command is that it doesn't cast any unwanted shadows and all the shadows are lighted evenly, no matter how distant from the lens.

You can correct overexposed highlights with the Adjust Backlighting command. This situation occurs when foreground objects are lit from behind, and you increase the exposure to bring the foreground objects out of shadow, which overexposes and washes out the background.

Why Do I Want More Detail in the Shadows and Highlights?

When shadows appear too dark and highlights are too bright, an unnatural lighting effect results. Without detail, the eyes perceive these areas as only shapes, which tends to flatten the sense of depth, form, and perspective. Restoring details in an image helps define the forms and adds dimension to the image, and produces the image you meant to shoot. The balance of detail in shadow and lighter areas allows the eyes to move freely throughout the picture with comfort and continuity.

How Do I Get More Detail?

Use the Photoshop Elements Fill Flash command to bring out details in shadow areas.

1. Choose Enhance | Adjust Lighting | Fill Flash. The Adjust Fill Flash dialog box appears.

2. Check Preview so that you can immediately see the result of your adjustment in the image window.

3. Drag the Lighter slider to the right to lighten the shadows. An example of this effect is shown in Figure 9-7. Since you can see the result instantly, simply stop when you like the result.

4. Adjust the Saturation slider to intensify or subdue the color in the filled shadow areas.

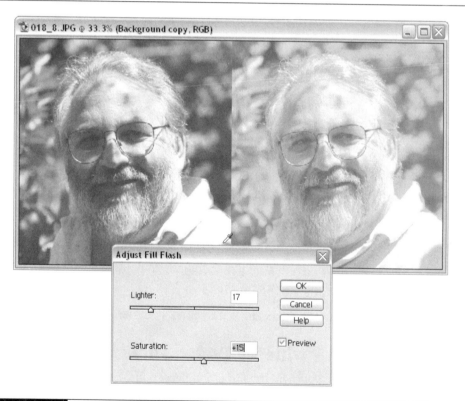

FIGURE 9-7   Before (left) and after using the Fill Flash command

FIGURE 9-8   Before (left) and after using the Adjust Backlighting command

Use the Photoshop Elements Adjust Backlighting command to bring out details in highlight areas.

1. Choose Enhance | Adjust Lighting | Adjust Backlighting.

2. Adjust the slider to the right to lighten the shadows. An example of this effect is shown in Figure 9-8 (above).

3. Check Preview to see the changes immediately in the image window.

62. Open Up Shadows with the Dodge Tool

When you *open up* a shadow, you lighten it and expose the detail that was hidden. This is similar to opening the pupil of your eye to see better in the dark.

Dodging is a traditional darkroom technique. During exposure, parts of the photographic paper can be shaded to lighten those areas. The Dodge tool produces the same effect but works in a different way. Instead of holding light back, it adds light to darker pixels to raise their luminance. The tool is useful when you want to lighten only selected detailed areas of an image with a hand-brushed technique. Figure 9-9 shows an image changed by using the Dodge tool.

How Do I Use the Dodge Tool to Open Up Shadows?

Here's how to use the Dodge tool in Photoshop Elements:

1. Open the image in Photoshop Elements.

2. Choose the Dodge tool from the Toolbox.

3. Adjust the brush size and Exposure Value on the Options bar. The Exposure Value controls how fast the effect builds up with multiple passes. Raising the Exposure Value to more than about 12 percent often causes streaking and grayed-out areas.

4. Choose Shadows, Midtones, or Highlights from the Range menu. The Range determines the luminance range where the effect is most dominant.

5. Paint over the areas you want to lighten, building up the effect with multiple passes over the same area.

FIGURE 9-9 The cat's eye on the left was dodged using midtone and highlight image-editing options.

63. Use a Soft Light Blend Mode Layer

Soft Light is the name of a blend mode (see Tip 84 in Chapter 12 for more on blend modes). By setting up a layer with a Soft Light blend mode, you can achieve some effective dodging and burning in an image. *Burning* is a traditional darkroom technique. During exposure, parts of the photographic paper are exposed to more light to darken those areas. The Burn tool produces the same effect but works by subtracting luminance from lighter areas.

How Do I Use This Blend Mode Tool to Open Up Shadows?

The Soft Light blend mode burns in the underlying pixels if the brush brightness is lighter than 50 percent luminance (middle gray) and dodges the underlying pixels if the color in the brush is darker than 50 percent luminance. You can switch from dodge to burn by switching from black to white brush colors or shades of gray to reduce the power of the effect. Choosing middle gray will have no effect. Soft Light has no effect on areas that are pure white and pure black.

Here's how to use the Soft Light method of dodging and burning:

1. Open an image in Photoshop Elements.

2. From the Palette well, open the Layer Palette.

3. Create a new layer by clicking on the middle icon at the bottom of the Layer Palette. A new transparent layer will appear.

4. Set the layer attribute to Soft Light mode from the drop-down menu just below the Layer tab.

5. Set the Background and Foreground colors to black and white, respectively.

6. Choose the Paintbrush from the Toolbox. Size is arbitrary. Set the opacity at 100 percent. Lower the opacity to reduce the effect.

7. Use white to bring out detail in shadows and black to bring out detail in highlights.

NOTE   *You can press X to switch from foreground to background color. Use shades of gray instead of black and white to control the power of the effect. The brush does not affect black or white in the image.*

64. Create Your Own Shallow Depth-of-Field

Depth-of-field is the distance in front of and behind the center of focus in which everything is in reasonably sharp focus. (See Tip 15 in Chapter 3 for more information.)

Why Do I Want to Change the Depth-of-Field?

Details in the foreground or background can often act as visual interferences to the main subject. Depth-of-field is normally changed by adjusting the aperture of the lens, but most digital cameras keep in relatively sharp focus almost everything that's more than a couple of feet away from the camera. The result is that, without the aid of a little digital image-editing magic, it's very hard to keep interest focused on the subject by letting the foreground and background blur out-of-focus.

So what do you do to get rid of the clutter when this occurs? Obscuring these unwanted details with the Gaussian Blur Filter allows the viewer to focus on what you intended and lets the other visual details act as a backdrop. In other words, you've created the illusion that you've shortened the depth-of-field of the shot. Blurring the detail can even enhance the main subject. This process mimics much of what your brain actually does when you are focusing with your eyes. For instance, when you are focusing on someone's face, the background is blurred. You suppress the extraneous details surrounding the subject and accentuate the facial details.

Figure 9-10 shows an image before and after the Blur Filter is used.

FIGURE 9-10   Before (left) and after the Blur Filter is used on selected background areas.

How Do I Change the Depth-of-Field?

Use the Photoshop Elements Selection tools along with Blur Filter to achieve this effect.

1. Open the image in Photoshop Elements.

2. Use one or more of the Selection tools to select the areas of the image that you want to keep sharp. (The Lasso and Magic Wand tools were used in Figure 9-10. See Chapter 11 for more on selections.)

3. Invert the selection so that it is selected instead of the subject. Choose Select | Inverse or press COMMAND-I (Mac) or CTRL-SHIFT-I.

4. Choose Selection | Feather.

5. In the Feather dialog box, change the Feather value (see Tip 78 in Chapter 11) to increase the area at the edge of the selection that will smoothly transition so you don't end up with a hard edge.

6. Choose Filters | Blur | Gaussian Blur. The Gaussian Blur dialog box appears. Adjust the slider to change the amount of blur.

7. Click OK to apply the blur to the selection.

Chapter 10

Retouching Your Images

Photographs rarely come out perfect; that's why it is common practice for photographers to go in afterward and use image-editing software to tweak their photos so that they include and express just what they want them to. This chapter introduces image-editing techniques that can help you retouch your pictures and get them close to perfection. The extent to which you take retouching is entirely up to you—it can be as simple as covering over a few blemishes or as complex as giving someone a facelift or a hair-color change.

65. Fix Red Eye in Your Image Editor

When an internal flash is used, it typically aims the light directly at the person being photographed so the light actually bounces off the retina and back at the camera. This will produce pupils that are bright red in the photograph. This is called *red eye*, and it makes your subjects look like they're ready for Halloween.

How Do I Use Image-Editing Software to Eliminate Red Eye?

Photoshop Elements makes it easy to eliminate red eye from your portraits by providing a special tool called Red Eye Brush.

1. Open the image in Photoshop Elements.

2. From the Toolbox, choose the Red Eye Brush tool. The Red Eye Brush Options bar will appear. Choose a brush size and style that is appropriate for the area you are working in.

3. Because in most instances you will be changing the color in the pupil, the default replacement color on the Options bar is black. The Current Color box shows you the color the cursor is currently over. You can set the Sampling option to be First Click or Current Color—First Click picks up the color from the first position you start painting from, and Current Color uses the current foreground color as the reference. The Tolerance level determines how many shades of the sampling color (in most cases red) will be affected by the brush. You want the Tolerance level to be set high enough to affect them all. Place the cursor over the red part of the pupil so you can choose the sampling color that determines which colors are replaced or use the Eyedropper tool to make the red the current foreground color.

4. With the Red Eye Brush, move your cursor over the region to be changed. Choose the sampling color, observing the Current Color box on the Options bar.

5. Drag to start replacing color over the red area. The brush will change the color but not the luminance value of the pixels, so the detail in the eye will remain unchanged. Adjust the Tolerance and resample as necessary until all the red is gone.

> **NOTE** *You can use the Red Eye Brush to change the color of other parts of the image as well. Just sample in other areas or choose a foreground color by changing the Sampling option to the Current Color. You could use it to change the color of someone's eyes or of the flowers in a dress pattern.*

66. Eliminate Small Annoyances with the Clone Stamp Tool

The Clone Stamp tool is one of the handiest image-editing tools ever invented, and you will use it time and time again. Do you have blemishes, specs, unwanted doodads, glitches, or just plain junk in your photos? The Clone Stamp tool can make all these pesky little things disappear.

The word *clone* means to reproduce with absolute fidelity. The Clone Stamp tool copies a section of pixels from one area of a picture to another. This section can be from the same image, another layer, or another image entirely. The Clone Stamp tool allows you to set a source and then target an area within the image and reproduce the pixels from the source to where you are painting.

Why Do I Need to Clean Up My Images?

What if you didn't have time to get every piece of garbage off the lawn before you took the shot, or Aunt Clara had a speck of food on her wonderful smile? These might have been perfectly good photographs, had it not been for a few small flaws that marred the shots. Don't panic. The Clone Stamp tool provides an efficient way of removing all sorts of visual clutter and defects in your photo with great precision. An unwanted item can be removed by copying an acceptable similar area over the defective area.

How Do I Use the Clone Stamp Tool to Edit?

Using the Clone Stamp tool, you can target certain areas of an image to use as a source for a brush stroke. The tool "paints" with the pixels that are part of the set target source. For example, to fix some blemishes on a subject's face, you could set the source target on a clear section of skin and then move the tool over the blemishes, painting over them with a copy of the clear skin at the source, and the blemishes would be covered. Setting the tool opacity at a lower setting would allow you to blend in the skin gradually so it looks seamless (see Figure 10-1).

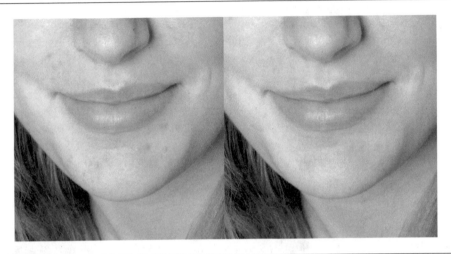

FIGURE 10-1 Before (left) and after using the Clone Stamp tool to cover blemishes

Also, be sure to clone from an area that is the same color and brightness as the area immediately surrounding the blemish you want to cover. Otherwise, you'll just create a different kind of blemish.

Here's how to use the Clone Stamp tool:

1. Open the image in Photoshop Elements.

2. Choose the Clone Stamp tool from the Toolbox.

3. Set the brush size, opacity, and blend mode on the Options bar.

4. Select Aligned if you want the sampled area to move with the tool. This keeps the source area in close proximity to the painted area so you can use similar local detail as a source.

   Deselect Aligned if you want the sampled area to reposition to the original target every time you stop and start painting again. Use this option when you want to keep reusing the same source image area in a number of locations.

5. Position your cursor over the source and OPTION-click (Mac) or ALT-click. You will see the cursor change to a target, indicating that the source has been set.

6. Position the cursor where you want to begin painting with the Clone Stamp tool and start painting. You will see the source location, indicated by a crosshair, maintain a constant distance and orientation as you move the Clone Stamp tool. The crosshair indicates the pixel area that the tool is using to paint with.

67. Smooth Out the Wrinkles

Wrinkles can occur in any surface—skin, cloth, earth, and water, for example. Anything with an undulating surface that might look better smoothed applies here.

Why Should I Get Rid of Wrinkles?

People have been looking for the Fountain of Youth for eons, but nobody has been able to find one—until now. Using some simple smoothing and blending techniques, you can make wrinkles and hard texture vanish, adding a youthful texture to a face of any age.

How Do I Use Image-Editing Software to Remove Wrinkles?

Welcome to the world of digital plastic surgery. Figure 10-2 shows what can be done with a good image-editing program. The trick with this method is to blur a copy of the image so that the very dark and very light tones in the copied image blend together, eliminating deep and high areas of the surface. This smoothed image acts as a source in painting in the wrinkles with an "erase-through" process.

FIGURE 10-2   Before (left) and after the wrinkles around his eyes and forehead and blemishes on his cheek were blended away

Following is a clever technique that will take 20 years off an aging face:

1. Open the image you want to "rejuvenate."

2. Duplicate the base layer two times. Select the second layer.

3. Choose Filter | Blur | Gaussian Blur. (I used a setting of around 20 to get a good spread and mix of light and dark tones in Figure 10-2.) Experiment with settings to get the best spread for your subject. Also, the exact setting will be dependent on the size of the image and the magnification of the wrinkles.

4. Choose Filter | Noise | Add Noise. The setting should be around 5. Choose Uniform and Monochromatic.

5. Select the third layer. You will use the Eraser tool to erase through the image on this layer to reveal the blurred image below. By erasing the wrinkle areas, you blend in the smoothed values from the image below, which makes the wrinkles diminish significantly.

6. Choose the Eraser tool from the Toolbox and set the brush size small enough to work in the wrinkles with a small amount of overlap. Set the opacity such that the effect builds up gradually.

NOTE *You'll get the best results using a pressure-sensitive pen so that you can vary the transparency of the erased areas by the amount of pressure you put on the tip of the pen.*

68. Draw Attention to the Eyes

People make the most significant contact with another person through that person's eyes, so the more expressive and noticeable you make the eyes, the more impact the photo is likely to have. Focusing attention on the eyes is a powerful tool to hold the viewer's attention and draw the viewer into the subject. With a few simple adjustments, you can increase the vibrancy of the subject's eyes to make a portrait captivating and more alive.

How Do I Use Image-Editing Software to Accomplish This?

To accentuate the eyes, you need to brighten the whites, darken the outer edge of the iris, and lighten the inner iris by boosting contrast. Boosting the color saturation of the iris can add punch, too, but be careful not to push it too far or it will look unnatural. (See Figure 10-3 for an example of a well-done enhanced eye.)

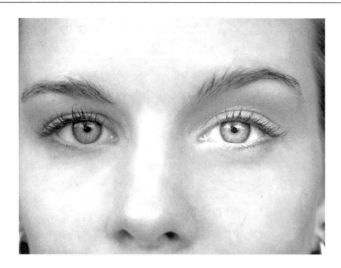

FIGURE 10-3   The eye on the right is much more captivating after being enhanced.

Here's how to enhance a subject's eyes:

1. Select the eye area with one of the selection tools that allows you to make a freeform selection, so that you don't include any more surrounding skin than necessary. Include the edges of eyelids and lashes. Also, make a separate selection around the eyebrows. (See Tip 77 in Chapter 11 for more on selections.)

2. Choose Select | Feather. Set the value large enough to get a gradual transition so any effects blend into the face seamlessly.

3. Choose Enhance | Adjust Brightness/Contrast | Brightness/Contrast. Adjust the sliders to raise contrast and brightness.

4. Select just the iris area with the Lasso tool and feather the edges for a smooth transition.

5. Choose Enhance | Adjust Color | Hue/Saturation. Adjust the saturation up to boost the color of the iris.

NOTE   *The key here is to accentuate but at the same time be subtle. If you push the enhancement too far, the eyes will look fake, and that will defeat the whole purpose.*

69. Sharpen Eyes and Other Specific Areas of the Image

Before you can understand sharpening, you need to look at what causes softening. A sharp edge has a quick transition in contrast from one side of the edge to the other. This means that if you have a black edge on a white background, for example, it will go from white to black with few or no levels of gray in between, making the edge appear hard (sharp). If you take the same edge and transition it gradually so that many levels of gray are used, it will appear softer, like a fold or ripple.

When an image has mostly soft edges, it can appear to be slightly out of focus. To bring the image into tighter focus, you can use special routines to increase the contrast of the edges by removing some of those transitional colors.

Why Would I Want to Sharpen Specific Areas?

Sharpening detail brings the image into focus and produces a more vibrant and powerful photograph. It is also more relaxing for the eyes of the viewer, which have to work harder to bring blurry or soft images into focus. This will annoy viewers, even if they don't understand why. Sharper detail also means more depth and definition of form, and it sets off the distinction of shape and color with more power. Clearly delineated edges and detail add more force to your composition and allow the image to come off the paper and reach out to the viewer. The sense of realism is greatly enhanced.

How Do I Use Image-Editing Software to Sharpen Detail?

To sharpen key detail, use the Unsharp Mask filter. This Filter preserves the smooth transitions in the image and focuses its sharpening routines to areas of the image that are properly perceived as edges. This prevents unsightly pixel brightening in the middle of areas that should be smooth, which can be the byproduct of standard sharpening filters. Unsharp Mask provides a number of controls that determine which edges get sharpened and the extent to which they are sharpened. Figure 10-4 shows an image before and after the Unsharp Mask Filter was used.

Here's how to increase the sharpness of edge detail in an image:

1. Open a slightly blurred image in Photoshop Elements.

2. Choose Filter | Sharpen | Unsharp Mask.

3. Move the Amount slider to increase or decrease the contrast of the edges that are being sharpened.

4. Move the Radius slider to increase the area of sharpening effect around the edge.

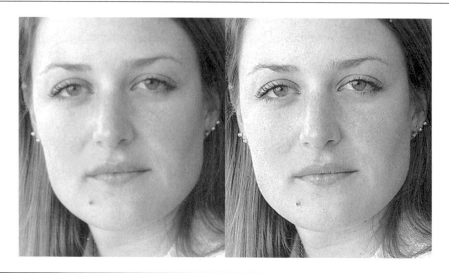

FIGURE 10-4   Before (left) and after the Unsharp Mask filter was used to bring out detail

5. Move the Threshold slider to determine how different the pixels need to be in value to be considered an edge.

6. View the results in the preview window. When you achieve the look you want, click OK.

70. Spread Highlights to Achieve Glamour Blurring

The soft glow that appears around glamour shots can give the subject an ethereal quality. That glow is produced by spreading out the highlights of the image, adding an aura of light to the subject. This can be achieved with a special lens and lighting in a professional studio, or you can achieve it with your digital photographs by using some simple software techniques.

What Are Highlights?

Highlights are the bright points of light in a scene that indicate reflection of the light source. They can brighten up reflections in chrome or general reflections that come from light-colored surfaces, such as a white shirt. Highlights are the brightest colors in the photo and are key to interpreting the type and quality of the light source. Sharp, intense highlights indicate a strong focused light such as a spotlight, while soft, diffused highlights indicate a more general light source such as an overcast day or flourescent lighting.

Why Would I Want to Spread the Highlights?

By softening the highlights, you can change the nature and quality of the lighting in the scene to be soft and more intimate. It's like lowering the dimmer switch or adding a special shade to make the lighting more romantic.

How Do I Use Glamour Blurring to Spread Highlights?

1. Open the image you want to glamour blur.

2. Duplicate the image to one more layer. Select the second layer.

3. Choose Filter | Distort | Diffuse Glow. Move the slider to a value that spreads the highlights nicely, eliminates most edge detail, and makes the skin glow. Be sure to drag the Graininess slider to its lowest setting. When you like what you see in the preview window, click OK.

4. In the Layers Palette, choose Soft Light from the Blend mode menu.

5. Make sure the diffused layer is selected (highlighted) and drag the Opacity slider until you feel you have the right balance between the glow effect and the original image (see Figure 10-5).

FIGURE 10-5   From left to right—the original image, the image with enhanced highlights, and the merged image after adding the glow

71. Convert Color Photos to Black-and-White

Fundamentally, in the digital world, there is no difference between a black-and-white image and a color image with no color saturation. Every color appears as a pure gray in the black-and-white image. A color is *pure gray* when the color channels are all equal in strength. For instance, an RGB (Red, Green, and Blue) color value of 128, 128, 128 would give you a midtone gray; 0, 0, 0 would give you black.

When you change a color image to black-and-white, you move the RGB values to gray while maintaining the overall brightness of each color. You can convert a black-and-white image to a grayscale image, which strips out the color information completely and stores only the luminance level information, which decreases the size of the file. Converting your color images to black-and-white also teaches you about how light works in your photographs, because you can see the pure light values more clearly.

NOTE
Grayscale files cannot be colorized unless they are converted back to RGB.

Why Would I Want to Change a Color Photo to Black-and-White?

On the practical side, you may find it necessary to change a color photo to black-and-white for publication, to produce photocopies, or to create faxable documents. Converting color photos to black-and-white and then adjusting the brightness and contrast can increase the quality in reproduction, because some colors don't translate well when photocopied in black-and-white.

For a more subjective reason, black-and-white photos can be used to express a unique feeling and quality. By eliminating the color components, the image focuses on the value of the light and the interplay of shapes. If you are looking for an abstraction of reality, black-and-white helps detach the subject matter from the everyday.

How Do I Convert the Image?

■ Load a color photograph in your image editor, and then open the Saturation control. Reduce the saturation to zero and watch the color photo become black-and-white.

Another way to accomplish this task:

■ Choose Enhance | Adjust Color | Remove Color.

And here's a third alternative:

■ Choose Image | Mode | Grayscale.

You may notice that some colors that looked comparatively different in color may look similar in gray. This happens because even though the color values were different, the luminance values were close. You can adjust for some of these problems by changing contrast and levels to accentuate some of the differences in shades.

72. Color Tone Black-and-White Photos

Color toning is a process of tinting the image with a single hue. It is also called *colorizing*. If you were to shine a light on the photo through a colored gel, as is used in stage lighting, it would give the appearance of color toning. Color toning is an ambient effect that changes the overall color of the image. Color toning can give the appearance of an old-style photo with sepia tones, or it can be more upbeat by adding brighter and more radical color changes. It is an easy effect that adds another dimension to an image.

Why Would I Want to Color Tone Black-and-White Photos?

■ Color toning is an easy way to achieve an antique look in an image. Old photographs often have a brownish cast to them. You can simulate that using color toning.

■ Color toning can also be used as a way of differentiating images used for a menu on the Web.

■ By color toning your black-and-white photos, you can add another level of expression to accentuate a mood without giving up the simple but powerful quality of black-and-white images.

How Do I Color Tone an Image?

Open the image you want to color tone. It doesn't need to be in black-and-white to begin with, as this process will convert the image to black-and-white at the same time it colorizes it.

Try This: **Focus on Color**

Color toning can be used as a powerful tool for altering parts of a black-and-white image so they stand out from the background. Select areas you want to accentuate, then color tone the selected areas. This will focus the viewers attention on the color-toned portions of the image. This technique can be used on color photos also.

1. Choose Enhance | Adjust Color | Hue/Saturation.

2. Check the Colorize option, and you will see the image change to a color-toned image of the hue selected on the top slider.

3. Move the Hue slider to change the color tone.

4. Click OK when you're done.

73. Hand Color Black-and-White Photos

Hand coloring is a process of colorizing individual areas of an image with a brush and transparent color. Hand coloring maintains tonal values as you paint the color. It is much like the effect of painting a watercolor wash over a pen-and-ink drawing.

NOTE   *The first color photographs were hand-painted black-and-white photos. Transparent oil paints were used to color these early photographs. Actually Marshall photo-coloring oils are still in wide use today, primarily by wedding and portrait photographers who want to give their images a classic and timeless look.*

Why Would I Want to Hand Color Black-and-White Photos?

Hand coloring can be used to create an interesting effect that mimics the hand-tinted photographs of years past, or to create the look of old postcards. You can scan old black-and-white photos and hand color them to achieve this affect. Relatives might find it exciting to see a scene from the distant past brought back to life in color, or you can use hand-colored photos to achieve an effect in a brochure or create an old-fashioned postcard.

You can choose to color portions of a photo to accentuate them or paint in every detail. When you are coloring by hand, you have precise control of where the color goes and how it should look. The choice of colors is up to you, so the whole process becomes much more about imagination and creativity and realizing your vision. If you have painting skills, this is a good opportunity to apply some of them to your photographic pursuits.

How Do I Hand Color Photos?

There are two basic ways to go about this. The first method described is layer-based. The advantage of using layers is that if you don't like the result, you can delete the layer and start over. You can also try several other effects of blending the colors with the underlying layer by changing to different layer blend modes.

1. Open the image you want to paint. If it is in color, convert it to black-and-white (see Tip 72 in this chapter).

2. Create a new layer and make it the active layer.

3. Set the layer mode to Color.

4. Choose the Paintbrush tool from the Toolbox. Adjust the size and style to match the detail you will be painting.

5. Set the Opacity value lower to build up the color more gradually.

6. Choose a foreground color. You will notice the color conforms to the tonal values of the underlying image, so you don't need to worry about shading.

7. Begin painting with the Paintbrush tool.

8. When you're satisfied with the image, you can save it.

The second method for hand coloring is faster, but doesn't offer you as much flexibility as the layer-based method:

1. Open the image you want to paint. If it is in color, convert it to black-and-white (see Tip 72 in this chapter).

2. Choose the Paintbrush tool from the Toolbox. Adjust the size and style to match the detail you will be painting.

3. Choose the colors you want to use, then change the brush's blend mode to Color in the brush's Options bar. Then, when you stroke with the brush, the brightness values of the black-and-white image remain the same, but the picture is tinted with the current foreground color.

4. When you're satisfied with the image, you can save it.

74. Correct Perspective Distortion

If you hold your camera at an odd angle while shooting vertical or horizontal objects, you can produce perspective distortion in your image. If the camera is not parallel to those objects while the shot is taken, it will distort the object by exaggerating the perspective, causing it to look unnaturally squeezed at one end, as shown in Figure 10-6.

FIGURE 10-6   An example of perspective distortion

Why Should I Correct Perspective?

When you took the shot, you didn't see the image in such a contorted manner, so if you want your photo to reflect the scene accurately, you'll want to fix this distortion.

Although there are artistic uses for purposefully distorting scenes, most of the time it is a problem. Your brain compensates for this distortion every time you tilt your head to look up at a building. This ability to compensate is what makes our brains different from the camera's brain. If you want your final image to match how your brain thinks an image should look, you will need to do some sort of correction.

How Do I Correct Perspective Distortion?

The process of correcting perspective distortion involves stretching or distorting the image to re-form it back to the way it should look. Some wonderful tools are available to make this a fairly easy process.

Here's how to correct perspective distortion:

1. Open an image that needs correcting.

2. In the Layers Palette, double-click the background layer's Name bar. The New Layer dialog box appears.

3. Enter a new name for the background layer and click OK. This will turn the background layer into an ordinary layer. Background layers cannot be transformed.

4. Choose Image | Transform | Distort. The transform box will appear with handles on all sides and all corners.

5. Click and drag the corner handles to correct the distortion. You'll want to make vertical lines parallel with the sides of the image frame and the horizontal lines parallel with the top and bottom edges, if possible. You may have to pull more than one handle to achieve this. Figure 10-7 shows how this process looks.

6. When you have corrected the distortion to your liking, click the Commit button in the Options bar (the big check mark on the right side) or press ENTER to render the transformation.

7. If necessary, use the Crop tool to trim any slanted edges that result. If you have dragged all the lines outside the Canvas (work area), this will not be a problem.

FIGURE 10-7   The distortion transformation handles being positioned so the image appears correctly proportioned

Chapter 11

Creating a New Reality
with Composites

So far, you've learned what you can do to a single photograph to make it better, sharper, and brighter. Now it's time to enter the world of *composites*, the technique of combining multiple digital images into one. You're leaving conventional photography behind to immerse yourself in the world of computer imaging, where your imagination knows no bounds. At the core of compositing are the almighty layers that let you stack many images or parts of images in endless combinations and interlayer effects.

75. Stack Components on Layers

Layers are a function of the Layers Palette. You can use layers to stack a number of images or pieces of images within a single document and work each layer individually. Imagine a number of horizontal panes of glass that are stacked with a little space in between, so you can slip in image transparencies to rest on the surface of each layer. You can place images on the pane at the bottom, and then work your way up by stacking other images on other layers above. Some layers may include portions of images, so if you look down on the stack, you can see the stacked images below, where partial images let lower layers show through, forming a composite image. Digital layering is a complex process by which layers can change their transparencies and blend with other layers below in many ways.

The *components* represent all the pieces of a composite image that fit together to make the final image you see in the image window—text, gradients, textures, shapes, images or pieces of images, hand-drawn art, scans, special effects, or layer styles. You typically separate components into individual layers in an image.

Try This: Make a Simple Composite from Film

An easy way to understand the idea of components is to stack two or three slides or negatives (make sure they are not too dark) on a light box or in a slide viewer. The image you will see is a combination of all the stacked images—a *composite* of the *components*, which are the images on the individual pieces of film.

Why Should I Stack Images in Layers?

Layers keep components separate, and stacking keeps them in order, from background on the lowest layer to foreground on the uppermost layer. When creating a composite, you are blending images from different sources. It is important that you carefully position, resize, and apply effects to blend the components into a unified composition. Stacking each component on a separate layer gives you maximum control over each part of the composite. If you are making a layer partially transparent, applying a blend mode, or erasing parts of an image, the effect of these operations allows the lower layer(s) to show through in some way. You can reposition layers to see how this affects the composite image. Consider layers the ultimate light box.

NOTE   *If you adjust a layer to 50% opacity, it becomes like a sheet of tracing paper, showing the lower image while still showing the components on the active layer. This can serve as a handy reference for positioning and sizing.*

How Do I Use Layer Stacking to Create Composites?

To get familiar with using composites, you can stack a number of photographs that include elements you want to combine on layers in a single document. Don't worry about which images you choose, as this exercise is meant only to get your feet wet. Place the image you want to use as a background on the first layer. The image components that you will cut from lower layers will be placed in the upper layers.

NOTE   *If you don't like something you've done, remember that you can always move the layers around, partially erase them, change their transparency, and change the way their colors interact with layers below them.*

Cut out the image components from the background layers so you have a number of layers with image components on transparent backgrounds. An image component could be a picture of anything—a head, a flower, or a body of water, for example. The challenge is finding pieces that go together well and then figuring out how to merge them to make the image look like a single shot. That can take a little practice.

Figure 11-1 shows an interesting effect created by merging two images to create a composite.

 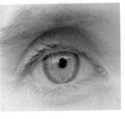 

FIGURE 11-1   A composite of the two images on the left created the image on the right.

Transparency can be achieved by erasing unwanted portions of the image with the Eraser tool or by creating a selection and cutting away portions (see Tip 77 later in this chapter). Using selections will give you the added advantage of being able to feather the edge of an object, which makes merging components easier (see Tip 78 later in this chapter). You can hide layers by clicking the eye icon next to the layer in the Layers Palette. Making a layer active allows you to edit the images on that layer alone, so you can move from one component to another until you get them all edited properly.

NOTE   *You can make duplicate layers of components and then make the original layers invisible before you start to modify the duplicate layers. This way, you can go back to the original layer if your experiments go astray.*

76. Make Collages Using Layer Transparency

A *collage* is a form of composite that is unique in a stylistic sense. In traditional art, a collage is made up of image pieces that have been pasted together to form a conglomerate of images. The collage artist doesn't attempt to blend together these images in a seamless manner to create the appearance of a unified subject, but rather revels in diversity and contrast. Collages are viewed as visual conversations. The viewer's eye wanders around, picking up bits and pieces of the image just as the artist did when it was created.

Much of compositing is dedicated to producing unified images that you might not even suspect had multiple sources. Collages, on the other hand, make no bones about being loudly diverse. You can create a digital collage by using composite techniques to piece together all sorts of art and objects. You collect the objects with your camera and paste them together with your computer.

How Does Layer Transparency Help Me Create Collages?

Because collages are made up of pieces of all shapes and sizes, it is common practice to lay them out so they overlap each other. To stay true to that way of working, you can cut out all the components from their backgrounds and place them on transparent layers. Transparent layers allow you to place objects on separate layers and the transparency lets you see where they overlap, like those shown in Figure 11-2. You can move around the layers to change the positioning of the image objects and you can change the stacking order of the layers. You can also transform the objects on individual layers so that they can be any size and proportion in relationship to the objects on the other layers. The combination of stacking and moving opaque objects on transparent layers and of being able to transform those objects makes it possible to get exactly the collage composition you have in mind.

FIGURE 11-2 These image objects were cut out of other photographs and pasted into layers in one document to create a collage.

How Do I Use Transparency to Create Collages?

Here's how to create multiple-image objects with transparent backgrounds:

1. Open the image you want to cut out.

2. From the Toolbox, use one of the Lasso tools to outline the portion of the image you want to cut out. When you have finished the selection, choose Select | Inverse to invert the selection.

3. Cut the inverted selection (Edit | Cut). This leaves a transparent background around the image object.

4. Repeat this operation for all the image objects you want to include in your collage.

5. Copy all the images you have cut out and paste them into one document. As you paste them, they will be placed in unique layers with transparent backgrounds. You will be able to see the other objects through the transparent backgrounds of upper layers, as shown in Figure 11-2.

You can use the Eraser tool to create areas of transparency. You can also adjust the layer opacity, use blend modes, and add special effects (see Chapter 12). Anything you can photograph, scan, or draw can become part of your collage. And as a nice bonus, as long as you save your images in a format that preserves the layers, such as TIF or PSD, you can go back and modify your collage at any time. No glue to contend with.

Try This: Create a Family Scrapbook

For a nice family project, you can create a scrapbook in the collage style and add to it over time. You can create libraries of image objects by storing images on separate layers in documents that are named for the type of objects they contain. For example, you can name the library Family_Lib.TIF. You can drag these images from this document to any collage you are working on.

77. Make Use of the Power of Selections

Selections are one of the key components of any good image-editing program. A *selection* defines an area with an interactive tool and surrounds it with a boundary that is delineated by oscillating dashes that look like marching ants. Whenever you see those critters marching, you know they surround an active selection.

Selections limit the operation of almost every function of the editor to the area within the selection boundary. This containment lets you decide which selected areas of the image will receive specific operations. You can make selections with a number of tools in the Toolbox—the Elliptical and Square Marquee tools (geometric), Lasso tools (freeform or geometric), Brush Selection tool (freeform), and Magic Wand (freeform). (See Tip 79 in this chapter for more on the Magic Wand.)

Why Do Selections Help Me Work More Efficiently?

A selection lets you isolate any command or action in Photoshop to just that part of the image that's surrounded by the selection marquee. Selections let you quickly move, copy, crop, stretch, rotate, and cut any portion of an image. You can also copy the selection to a new layer or document, where it can become part of a composite. Selections help greatly in creating components. Selections can also be inverted, with the result that what was formerly outside the selection (that is, protected) becomes the inside of the selection.

Masks and selections serve the same purpose. The difference is that masks are selections that were saved to a special type of image layer, where they become grayscale images. Virtually all image-editing programs permit making selections. Only more advanced image-editing programs, such as Photoshop Professional and Painter, also support masks. The advantages of masks are that they can be altered with any of the Toolbox tools and that it's easier to alter portions of them in transparency.

How Do I Use Selections?

To select a portion of an image and make it a component in a composite, follow these steps:

1. Choose one of the section tools from the Toolbox, according to the shape of the area you want to define.

2. Select the object to define the outside edges of your selection. If you're using the Marquee tool, you will click and drag to make the selection. With the Lasso tool, you click and hold down the mouse button while you trace

the selection shape. You will see the moving dashes that define the border of the selection when you release the mouse button. The border will remain and the selection is active.

3. The selection can be repositioned while it is active. With the Marquee tool still active, place the cursor within the selection area. Drag it to a new location.

4. With the selection tool still active, right-click inside the selection area. From the pop-up menu, choose Copy Via Layer. A new layer with your selection appears in the Layers Palette.

5. Open a new document that is sized large enough to hold all of your components.

6. Select the Move tool from the Toolbox. Click the selection and drag it to the new document. You will see a duplicate of the selection copied to a layer in the new document.

Figure 11-3 shows a composite created by dragging objects to the new document. The apple and pear were cut from their background and dragged to a new document as a layer over the bananas. The bananas show because the area around the apples is transparent.

FIGURE 11-3   A composite created by dragging objects from one document to another

78. Blend Selections with Feathering

In conventional painting, *feathering* refers to a method of blending the paint from one area into another with fine bristles and soft, gentle strokes. Some painters actually use feathers to do this. The effect is much the same in the digital world, but you don't use a feather; you use the Feather command. The Feather command value determines how the edge of a selection transitions to the surrounding area. If you use no feather value, the selection will have a hard edge. The higher the feather value, the wider the area of soft transition at the edge of the selection. Figure 11-4 shows the effect of feathering a selection.

Why Should I Feather Selections?

Feather selections when you want to blend selections into a new background. This effect causes the merged images to look more natural. Feathering is also useful if you have designated an area of an image for enhancement, such as someone's eye, and you want the effect to blend back into the face around the eye so it appears seamless.

NOTE *Feathering edges to a transparent background produces edges with variable transparency built in, so it will blend easily with almost any background.*

FIGURE 11-4 A selection that has been feathered with a value of 30 (left), and a feathered selection pasted into another image (right)

How Do I Feather a Selection?

1. Open an image from which you want to cut a selection.

2. Choose one of the selection tools from the Toolbox.

3. Select the area with the selection tool.

4. Choose Select | Inverse to invert the selection. You will see the selection border reposition.

5. Cut the inverted selection to make the area you originally selected transparent.

6. Choose Select | Inverse again to reselect the original image.

7. Choose Select | Feather. The Feather dialog box will appear. Adjust the value to indicate the pixel dimension of the area you want to soften. The border of the selection will smooth slightly when you feather it.

8. Drag the image. When you move the image, it will feature translucent edges that blend to the colors in any background.

79. Select Complex Areas with the Magic Wand

The term *magic* is not so farfetched for this ingenious little tool. The Magic Wand is a selection tool designed to select areas of an image based on similar color. The range of color is controlled by a tolerance value that you set. You can use the Magic Wand to select an area of sky, for example, or to select the petals of a yellow flower—the entire object will be selected as long as the colors in the object are fairly consistent. This saves you the time (and anguish) of tracing an outline by hand.

Why Should I Use the Magic Wand?

In many instances, the Magic Wand can make selections that are next to impossible to do by hand, at least by any sane person. The Magic Wand lets you select complex areas, such as pieces of sky between tree branches. Try making a similarly complex selection by hand, and you'll learn to appreciate this tool. The Magic Wand does not perform well in areas that have a lot of color variations, but it can work miracles if you want to select clear areas of well-defined color. Even if the Magic Wand doesn't do a perfect job, it can often take you 90 percent of the way.

NOTE

It is often much faster to make a selection by hand if the majority of the area you have to select is already selected. Then you can zoom in, and just edit the edges of the selection for precise detail. You do this in most programs by pressing SHIFT *while drawing with a selection tool when you want to add to the existing selection and* OPTION *(Mac) or* ALT *when you want to subtract from it.*

How Do I Use the Magic Wand?

Here's how to select an area of similar color with the Magic Wand:

1. Open an image in which you want to make a selection.

2. From the Toolbox, choose the Magic Wand tool.

3. On the Magic Wand Options bar, set the Tolerance value you think might work for the area you want to select. You can experiment with this value to get it right. The idea is to get the value close enough to choose only the pixels that are in the area of color you want to select. If you want the edge of the selection to be smooth, click the Anti-aliased option. If you want all the pixels in the area selected to be adjacent, choose Contiguous. If you are selecting areas between branches, as shown in Figure 11-5, turn off Contiguous so it will find all instances of the color range, even though they are separated.

NOTE

If you turn off Contiguous so that you can make a selection, like the sky through the gaps in leaves, you may pick up lots of other areas you didn't want to include. It's easy to get rid of the superfluous areas. Choose the selection tool, press OPTION *(Mac) or* ALT, *and make a loose selection around the areas you didn't really want included. Those areas will no longer be selected.*

4. Click in the area of color you want to select, and observe the selection the tool makes. If it is not to your satisfaction, you can adjust the parameters and try again until you get the selection to appear as you want. If the Magic Wand does not choose the entire area, you can SHIFT-click in the areas it hasn't chosen to add them to the selection. The selection can also be edited with the other selection tools.

FIGURE 11-5   This complex selection took only a few seconds with the Magic Wand.

80. Incorporate New Skies

You can use "sky replacement surgery" to insert some truly wild blue yonder, replacing a humdrum sky with a brand-new one of your choice.

Why Would I Want to Change the Sky?

Photographing skies can be problematic. Often they appear uninteresting in a shot, because Mother Nature happened to move in that fog on the day you wanted to shoot, or because the sky was a dull gray overcast. Haze, smoke, or even the time of day can make it difficult for you to get a sky to look interesting or to add to the composition. Skies often appear washed out in a shot because the exposure was set to capture the foreground detail, which overexposed the sky. It is a shame to throw out a perfectly good photo because the sky doesn't look appealing. Image editing can let you create a replacement sky in your photo and possibly rescue it from the scrap bin. You can see an example of changing the sky in Figure 11-6.

FIGURE 11-6   The new sky on the right matches the excitement and dynamics of the event.

How Do I Insert a New Sky?

Before you can insert good skies into blasé photos, you need to capture some good sky shots and store them into a "library of skies" to act as replacements. You can shoot interesting skies when the atmosphere is clear and the clouds are dynamic. Photograph clouds, moods, and colors that come with storms, sunsets, sunrises, and other interesting times at their optimum. Collect lots of sky photos so that you can easily match the direction of light on the landscape with the direction of light in the sky. If the two don't match, try horizontally flipping the sky shot.

Here's how to replace one sky with another:

1. Open the image you want to correct.

2. Choose the Magic Wand tool from the Toolbox.

3. From the Options bar, set the Tolerance level to 33 and adjust it as necessary. Raise the Tolerance value to increase the range of selection, and lower it to reduce the range. Try to choose a midrange value so the Magic Wand has the greatest latitude to capture the range of color above and below the reference pixel you selected. To do this accurately, you might want to use the Magnifying tool to see the pixels more clearly. Deselect Contiguous if the sky colors are not all adjacent.

4. Click the Magic Wand tool in the sky area. The marching ants boundary appears, indicating the areas the Magic Wand selected. If the selection is not satisfactory, adjust the settings and try again. If no settings get it just right, it may be necessary to take the best one and then adjust it with one

of the selection tools (see the previous tip in this chapter for more about refining Magic Wand selections).

5. Choose Select | Feather and the dialog box appears. Set the Feather value to 5 to soften the edges of selection and help the new sky blend in. Adjust the Feather value as necessary.

6. Create a new layer by clicking on the New Layer icon at the bottom of the Layers Palette.

7. Open a new document with the image of a sky you want to use as a replacement.

8. Choose Select | Select All.

9. Choose Edit | Copy to place the new sky on the Clipboard.

10. Return to the original document. Make sure you are on the new blank layer you created. Choose Edit | Paste Into. This will place a copy of the replacement sky within the bounds of the selection. You can use the Move tool to move the replacement sky selection around and use the transformation handles to resize it to fit the area. The Magic Wand selection now acts as a mask, allowing only the new sky to show through where your original selection was made.

81. Add Texture to Your Photos

Virtual textures are achieved by creating patterns of lights and darks that are perceived by your eye as a pattern of texture. When you apply a texture over an image, you are superimposing or compositing the light and dark patterns into the image, giving it the appearance of texture. It is basically an illusion. Of course, if you want real texture, you can always have prints made on textured papers—such as artist's canvas or watercolor paper.

Why Add Texture to a Photo?

Applying textural effects to your photographs can add visual interest and can also help blend components in a composite by providing a visual knitting of sorts. By adding a texture to areas of the photo, you can accentuate surfaces, such as stone, wood, or leather. This can take the form of enhancing a texture that is already there or adding a new one over an existing surface.

Photography is an exercise in illusion: you take a two-dimensional image and attempt to make the viewer believe it is really three-dimensional. Manipulating the rendering of light on form creates this illusion. The more of that illusion you add to the photograph, the more powerful the delineation and the more focused it becomes. Therefore, the photograph has more visual impact. Texture is key to defining the type of surfaces we are viewing. It is the visual cue the brain uses to say this is skin, or sand, or smooth silk. The textural quality of your photo can have a significant impact on the viewer's senses.

How Do I Create and Add Texture?

The easiest method for adding texture involves using the Unsharp Mask Filter (see Tip 69 in Chapter 10 for more about sharpening) to accentuate the detail at the edges in the picture. This works best for hard-edge textures such as the chipping paint shown in Figure 11-7.

A second method involves superimposing textured patterns over existing areas of the image. This is accomplished with texture filters found in the Filter menu. A number of texture filters are available. In the example shown in Figure 11-8, the Craquelure Filter was used over the entire image to enhance the surface details and add a cracked look to the gourds. The Texturizer Filter lets you choose a number of preset textures, such as canvas, sandstone, brick, and burlap. You can also add your own textures, which you can load from any PSD file.

FIGURE 11-7   The image on the right shows the result of sharpening the details to accentuate the textural qualities.

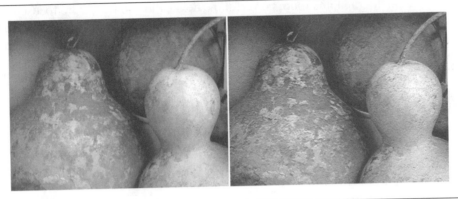

FIGURE 11-8   The original image (left) and the gourds with the Craquelure Filter applied (right)

If you want create a texture of your own to use in the Texturizer, you can create it in a separate document and save it as a PSD file. Keep the file size under 500×500 pixels for best performance. Keep in mind that textures need a fair amount of contrast (lights and darks) to work well and color is really not important. In fact, removing the color will help you adjust the contrast for the best result. You want a complete range from black to white.

NOTE   *You can create a whole library of textures by photographing real-life textures in macro mode and then editing them in Photoshop Elements to dramatize sharpness and contrast.*

When you open the Texturizer dialog box, choose Load Texture from the drop-down menu. Find the PSD file you saved, and load it. You will see the effect of your texture in the preview. Adjust the amount, the relief, and the direction of the light source to fine-tune it.

82. Match Grain

In conventional photography, the *grain* of film has to do with the fineness of the chemical particles that make up the color. When the negative is enlarged enough, you can actually see the particles, which give the picture a *grainy* look. With digital photographs, the graininess comes from noise ("visual static") in the circuits of the camera. The noise adds a color fluctuation that brands the file with a grain signature.

Why Do Grains Need to Match?

As you combine images and transform them with various tools, it is possible to come up with mismatches in grain. This occurs because as you alter areas of the image, you are stretching and smoothing the pixels and therefore changing the noise patterns. Because your eyes and brain are exceptional at recognizing patterns, these mismatches are very apparent. You want your changes to blend back into the image seamlessly, so you need to adjust the grain to camouflage the differences.

How Do I Go About Matching Grains?

The best tool for unifying textural mismatches is the Noise Filter. Although a Grain Filter is also available, this tool's results aren't as good as those of the Noise Filter, most of the time. You can try both filters and use the filter that works best for your situation.

Here's how to adjust the grain of a component to blend better into the original:

1. From the Layers Palette, make active the layer of the component you want to adjust.

2. Choose Filter | Noise | Add Noise. The Add Noise dialog box will appear, as shown in Figure 11-9.

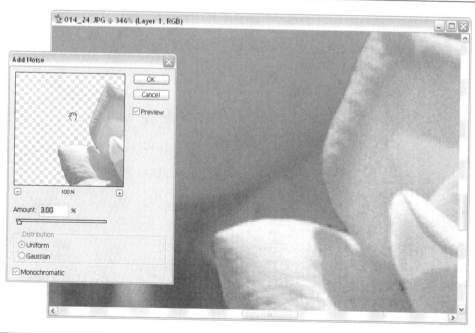

FIGURE 11-9 In the Add Noise dialog box, you can add noise to the rose in the foreground to make the textures match with the one behind.

3. Adjust the Amount slider to increase or decrease the amount of noise. Click the Uniform option to keep the distribution of noise constant over the area of effect. Click Gaussian to produce a high-contrast noise effect, and Monochrome will match the noise to the hue of the underlying pixels. With Monochrome turned off, you can produce RGB artifacts similar to the noise actually produced by the camera. Experiment with the setting until you get a good match to the original.

Chapter 12

Special Effects

This chapter is dedicated to some special techniques that take photographs beyond the everyday kind. You will learn how to add drama with lighting, blend photos to come up with unique looks, and even create your own weather effects. Special effects are fun to experiment with and easy to create.

83. Create Lighting Effects

Lighting effects are software routines that change the focus, quality, color, intensity, or spread of the lighting in the picture. You can accomplish these effects using filters or blends, or by hand painting your photos.

Why Would I Want to Create Lighting Effects?

Each type of lighting has its own unique look. Many professional photographers search for or create unusual lighting that will accent the subject of a photo shoot. The type and quality of the lighting can make or break a photograph in many instances.

Because perfect lighting isn't always available when the subject matter presents itself to be photographed, you can use image-editing software to add special lighting effects after the photo is taken. This opens up a wealth of creative opportunities, such as adding a soft spotlight to a portrait that guides the viewer's attention to a particular area of the picture, or changing the time of day. You can even change the season of a shot by altering the light to indicate a particular effect—create a cold look for winter or a warm look for summer. Lighting effects can add a sense of mood and drama to your photos.

How Do I Create Lighting Effects?

The Lighting Effects Filter is the most basic and easy-to-use tool in your image-editing tool kit. The filter allows you to create spot, directional, and flood lighting while controlling ambient (general) lighting at the same time. In Figure 12-1, I used a spotlight to focus a soft glow on the subject while darkening the general lighting to provide contrast.

To apply a lighting effect, choose Filter | Render | Lighting Effects to open the Lighting Effects dialog box shown in Figure 12-2.

In this dialog box, you'll see a circle and a radius line over the preview of your photo. The circle indicates the maximum diameter of the light and the radius line indicates the direction the light is shining. It is best to try and match the direction of the light to the existing light source, because the program needs to use the lights and darks to create the pseudo-lighting effect.

FIGURE 12-1   The Lighting Effects Filter can produce dramatic results as you can see with this before (left) and after.

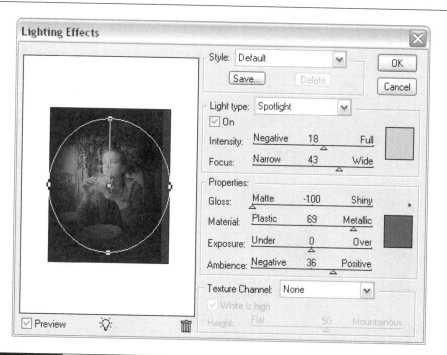

FIGURE 12-2   The Lighting Effects dialog box

The dialog box also includes the following features:

■ In the Style drop-down menu, you can choose from a number of preset lighting configurations. You can modify the settings after you choose a preset and save the setting you like as a new item.

■ Choose the light type from the Light Type drop-down menu: Spotlight, Directional, or Omni. Spotlight is focused lighting, Directional is flood lighting that has a light source, and Omni is similar to diffuse sunlight and doesn't have a strong directional component.

■ You can also adjust ambient lighting by using the Ambience slider in the Properties section near the bottom of the Lighting Effects dialog box. (Ambient refers to general atmospheric, or overall, lighting.)

■ You can set other lighting effects as well: Intensity affects the general brightness of the light, much like a dimmer switch. Focus works only for the spotlight and controls the area of illumination.

■ Back at the Properties section, the first two sliders (Gloss and Material) control the relationship between highlights and shadows to make objects look shiny or flat. Exposure is another way to control the intensity of the light.

■ The two colored squares on the right of the dialog box are used to set the color of the main light (top) and the ambient light. Click a square and the Color Picker will appear.

■ The bottom is the Texture Channel control. You can use this to create an embossed effect based on individual color channel values. The Texture Channel drop-down menu determines the color channel that will be texturized. The slider determines the depth of the texture. Check the White Is High box to make lighter areas appear raised. You can see this effect here:

■ Finally, you can add multiple lights by dragging the light bulb icon onto the preview screen at the left of the dialog box. You can set the parameters separately for each light. To remove a light, drag the center handle to the trash can.

84. Use Blend Modes for a Million Special Effects

Blend modes are one of the more powerful capabilities of Photoshop 7 and Photoshop Elements. Blend modes cause layers to interact and combine using mathematical formulas to create a variety of effects. These modes measure the differences between the layers in terms of color and luminosity and apply that information to the formulas.

The blend modes cause the layers to blend together in unique ways. You can darken, lighten, burn, dodge, create lighting effects, and also change hue, color, and intensity—to name a few. The results can sometimes be quite amazing and unpredictable.

Blend modes demand that you experiment with them, because no two combinations will produce the same results. The complex ways that they interact can produce millions of effects, partly because you can stack them up and have them cascade their effects through multiple layers. You can also combine blends with textures, gradients, and fills, giving you an even greater range. And if that's not enough, you can paint with blend modes, too.

You can find blend modes in the Mode menu in the Layers Palette and on the Options bar of the Paint tools.

Why Are Blend Modes So Powerful?

Blend modes can be used to change an image in radical ways. You can create interesting effects simply by placing images on multiple layers and selecting various blend modes for each layer. The greater the diversity in the images you choose to blend together, the greater the impact of the effect. Blend modes thrive on the differences between the images used, so don't be afraid to try combinations

---

Try This: Using Blend Modes with Fill Layers

One of the more powerful things you can do with blend modes is use them in conjunction with fill layers. If you choose Layer | New Fill Layer you'll get a submenu asking if you want the fill layer to be solid color, gradient, or pattern. Choosing one of these opens a dialog box that lets you set options for that type of fill (such as which color, gradient, or pattern you want to use and which variables you want to apply to them). As soon as you click OK, a layer that has been filled as prescribed appears immediately above the currently selected layer. You can then apply blend modes to this filled layer for an infinite variety of interesting effects.

that are a bit extreme. When you apply blend modes to multiple layers, the effects combine to increase the range of effects. The more layers you add, the more complex the mode interaction. General descriptions for each blend mode are in the help section in Photoshop Elements, but you will gain a greater understanding of this feature by loading the images and trying them out.

How Do I Use Blend Modes?

In Figure 12-3, I took a photograph of an iris and changed it into a soft outlined watercolor using blend modes and a few other tricks. This example gives you some idea of how you can use blend modes to create effects. This effect took only a few minutes to complete.

Here is how this is done:

1. Duplicate the background image twice and select the third layer.

2. Choose Filter | Stylize | Glowing Edges. Adjust the setting to get a nice, clean edge.

3. Choose Image | Adjustments | Invert to make the lines dark and the background light.

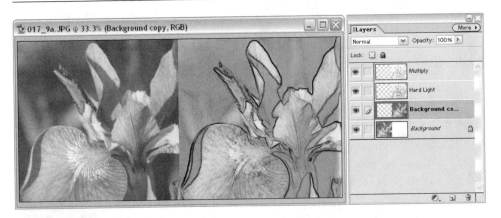

FIGURE 12-3   The iris on the left is transformed into a more artful image on the right with the use of blend modes.

Try This: View a Blend Mode Slideshow

Place two different images on separate layers. Select the top layer. Make sure you have dragged the Layers Palette out of the Palette well. Then you can press SHIFT-+ (plus sign) to cycle through all the blend modes and see how they affect the image.

4. Choose Enhance | Adjust Color | Remove Color so the outline is in grayscale.

5. From the Layers Palette Blend mode menu, choose Multiply. This will superimpose the dark outlines on the layer below.

6. Select the second layer.

7. From the Layers Palette Blend mode menu, choose Hard Light. Enter 50% in the Opacity field. The Hard Light blend mode uses a strong light effect to lighten the background image, while the lower opacity reduces the intensity of the effect.

The combination of the three layers gives the result shown in Figure 12-3.

85. Make Your Own Weather

Bet you didn't know that your desktop computer had a built-in weather generator. Your image editor can add some pretty wild weather effects to your photographs— rain, snow, fog, stormy clouds, and even lightning.

Why Would I Want to Add Weather Effects?

Weather special effects add a sense of mood and/or season, and they can make an image much more dramatic and interesting. Weather is dynamic and instills the photo with energy. It can give the viewer a sense of motion and a sense of the environment. Interesting weather is not always there when you are, so you can use special effects to make it happen when you want it, and you don't even have to get your camera wet.

How Do I Create Weather Effects and Add Them to My Images?

In Figure 12-4, you can see the same image with two distinct weather effects: lightning and snow. I wish I could show every weather effect available, but describing the snow effect will probably give you a pretty good idea of how to create a rain effect.

NOTE   *The lightning effect in Figure 12-4 was accomplished by painting the white by hand with a simple brush and then creating a layer underneath so I could paint in a blue glow, to give the photo that electric look.*

Here's how to create the snow effect:

1. Load an image that would look good with a little snow. Remember snow falls during a storm, so you should use a photo with cloud cover and a dark environment. And don't forget that you're going to create a winter scene, so no flowers should be in bloom or trees in leaf.

FIGURE 12-4   Two weather effects on the same scene

2.   The production of snow is a layered effect, so create three new layers. The first layer will be the smaller background snow, the second the middle-sized snow, and the last the foreground snowflakes. Each layer will show successively larger and more spread-apart snowflakes to maintain the perspective so that you get a sense of depth as you would in reality.

3.   From the Toolbox, choose the Paintbrush tool. Set the size at 2. Set the brush dynamics to Space: Maximum, Scatter: Maximum, Hardness: Maximum, and Jitter: 50%.

4.   Set the foreground color to white and the background color to a very light blue. The Jitter control will oscillate the colors between the foreground and background as you paint. This makes the snow look more natural. Reduce the layer transparency to 50%.

5.   Go to the next layer and enlarge the brush and continue to add flakes. Do the same with the third layer. You can use the Diffuse Filter, by choosing Filter | Stylize | Diffuse, to give the flakes a softer appearance.

NOTE   *You can create rain with almost exactly the same procedure except that raindrops would be transparent, smaller, and more elongated than snowflakes. They also tend to have a highlight where light reflects off the shiny drop. Of course, you can make it rain harder or lighter by increasing/decreasing the density and blur in the drops.*

86.   Combine Hand-Drawn Art with Photos

Hand-drawn art can be accomplished in two ways: the traditional way, by using pencil or paint on paper and then scanning the image into the computer; or the digital way, by using the drawing and painting tools provided in your image editor or paint program to create original works of digital art. Either one of these methods can be combined with a digital photograph to create an interesting effect.

Why Would I Want to Combine Art and Photos?

As you have certainly learned by now, digital photography is about moving beyond conventional boundaries and exploring whole new ways of creating photographic images. So the answer to this question is, why not? This could range from something as simple as a hand-scribbled annotation to the sophisticated world of digital *photopainting*. There is really that much latitude.

How Do I Combine Hand-Drawn Art with Digital Photos?

Combining digital photos and hand-drawn art is best accomplished by using layers and composite techniques. Most typically, the photograph is placed on a background layer and the drawing is done on a transparent layer above the photo. If you lower the drawing layer's opacity, you can still see the photo beneath even if you're using opaque paints. This is much like what animation artists do when creating cartoons. You could call this a "drawing-over technique"—in the animation industry it's called "onion-skinning" because onion-skin tracing paper is placed over the most recent frame of the cartoon. This allows the animator to properly position the elements in the next frame so that they will appear to move in the right degree and in the right direction.

In Figure 12-5, the tree was stylized from a photograph using the Threshold command and Sketch filters. The bird was drawn in by hand using the Paintbrush tool. This shows a simple, straightforward way to combine these two images.

FIGURE 12-5　　The hand-drawn bird adds a nice touch to the bare trees.

Another way to merge hand-drawn art with photos is to paint or draw digitally onto the photograph itself. This takes you into the world of photopainting. If you are ambitious, this kind of art can let you explore your creativity. As you can see in Figure 12-6, you can take the level of sophistication as far as you want. These images were created using a paint program. The still-life photograph was painted over with digital brushes that have the ability to move color around like a physical brush.

87. Combine Vector Art and Text with Photos

The key to understanding vector art is to think of it as outlined shapes. *Vector* art uses mathematics to define shapes by way of straight lines and curves. If you want to transform these shapes, you can let the mathematics reformulate the shape. Vector art is primarily used for clipart and text, because vectors make it possible to size these shapes without any degradation of edge detail. Vector art can be filled with color, gradients, and patterns, but it cannot easily render the kind of complex interior detail found in photographs. For that you need the power of individual pixels, accomplished through *raster* art. You can combine vector art and raster art by placing them on separate layers. When the layers are combined, the vector art must be converted to raster art.

FIGURE 12-6   This still life demonstrates what can be accomplished by combining hand-drawn techniques with photographs. The detail on the right gives a closer look at the digital brushwork.

NOTE   *Encapsulated PostScript (EPS) is a format that allows vector and raster art to reside in the same file and gets converted to pixels at the time of printing. This allows vector art detail to be maximized for the resolution of the printer.*

Why Would I Want to Combine Vector Art and Text?

Shapes and text maintain a higher quality when you create them as vector art. Keeping them in vector format maximizes their visual impact at the time they are printed. Photographs maintain more detail when they're created with the individual pixels of raster art. By combining the two forms, you get the highest possible quality—the best of both worlds. Anytime you add text to your image, you are adding vector art. A good portion of clipart in the form of shapes is also vector art. This is useful for captioning and annotating, and for greeting cards, brochures, and more.

How Do I Combine Vector Art with Digital Photos?

Photoshop Elements offers two ways to add vector art: via the Text tool or the Shape tool. To add clipart and text to a photograph, you will use layers to create the separate elements.

Figure 12-7 shows the results of combining text, shapes, and a photo to create an interesting greeting card image. The photograph used in this example is the background image, and the vector shapes and text reside in other layers above.

Here's how to add text to a photograph:

1. Open the image.

2. Choose the Text tool from the Toolbox.

3. In the Text Options bar, set font style, size, and color. Choose a color that will stand out against the background photo.

4. Click anywhere in the image to set a start point for the text entry. (Don't worry, because you can resize and reposition it later.) Type in the text, and it will appear on the screen. You can edit the text by clicking with the Text tool anywhere in the text. You can edit a block of text by clicking in the text with the Text tool and then dragging the mouse to select the text.

FIGURE 12-7 This greeting card took only a few minutes to create by combining text, shapes, and a photo.

5. If the text is the wrong size, you can enter a larger value in the Options bar. Or you can choose the Move tool, click the text, and then grab one of the bounding box handles and drag it to resize it. Hold down the SHIFT key to keep the resizing proportional.

Here's how to add custom shapes to a photograph:

1. Choose the Shape tool from the Toolbox.

2. From the Options bar, choose the Custom Shape icon, choose a Custom Shape from the Shapes menu, and then set the color.

3. Click and drag in the image window to create the shape. Use the bounding box handles to transform the shape.

NOTE

If you like, you can easily use text and shapes (both are drawn with vectors) to frame the contents of a photo. Size the photo to fit the current document and place it on the top layer of the document. Then create your shape or text (such as the name of the city). It will appear on a layer immediately above the photo. Choose Layers | Group with Previous. The photo will be hidden except where it shows through the letters or shapes.

Part III

Managing, Publishing, Printing, and Accessorizing

Chapter 13

Managing and Publishing Photos on the Web

Publishing photos to the Web has become a popular activity among photographers. Now that you have taken the first steps into digital photography, you will probably want to partake in this rapidly growing phenomenon. With a few simple tools and some understanding of how to get your photographs in the right format, you can start sending your images across the world in no time. Consider yourself lucky that you are getting into this now, because the tools designed to help have come of age and make Web publishing much easier than it used to be. By the time you finish this chapter, you will be on your way to showing off your photos in style to anyone with a Web connection.

88. Optimize Images for the Web

The World Wide Web is commonly referred to as the Internet, or just the Web. The Web is a global network that consists of many computers, called *servers*, that are distributed across the planet. These servers maintain software that allows all computers to communicate and transfer information. Computers with Web access are linked by phone lines, cable, fiber optics, and satellites forming a web of connections—thus the name. Each server has a unique address that identifies it, so it can be located in a matter of seconds. You can purchase your own unique domain name and space on a server from companies that host Web sites. You can use these servers to store and display your images to the Web.

Why Do I Need to Optimize for the Web?

All of the information displayed on your browser is transferred over electronic connections, such as your phone line. The larger the size of the file containing the information, the longer it takes to display on your system. Everyone knows what it's like to wait while a Web site takes forever to display. To avoid bogging down the system with slow-loading, gigantic files, you can optimize the information being sent to be as small as it can be, while still maintaining quality. You can use compressed data formats to reduce the size of the file and still allow for a decent image to appear.

Images, sound, and movies are some of the most data-intensive types of information you can send over the Web. If you were to send a full-sized digital photo over the Web, it could take more than an hour to display over an average connection speed of a regular modem.

How Do I Optimize Images for the Web?

Photoshop Elements, as well as other leading programs designed to create Web graphics, includes some automated tools that can help you get your images ready for Web display.

NOTE *Before you work on an image for use on the Web, be sure you resize it to the size at which it will appear on the Web. Otherwise, operations will be much slower than necessary and your optimization previews will be totally misleading.*

Following are the steps in optimizing a typical digital photo and saving it to a Web-ready format:

1. Open the image that you want to optimize for the Web.

2. Choose File | Save For Web. The Save For Web dialog box appears, as shown in Figure 13-1.

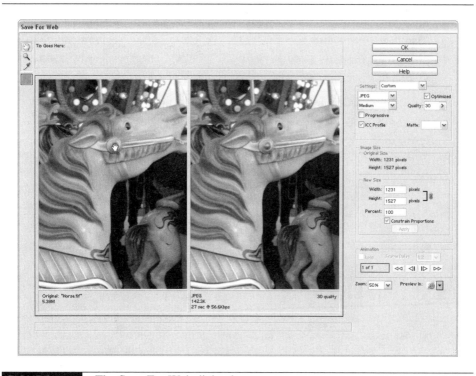

FIGURE 13-1   The Save For Web dialog box

Here, you choose how your image will be optimized and what format to use. The preview windows allow you to see before (left) and after images to evaluate the effects of compression and color reduction. In this exercise, you'll learn how to convert a high-resolution TIF photograph into a compressed JPEG file that loads quickly over the Web without losing too much quality. For now, we'll concentrate on the information in the Settings area of this dialog box.

3. In the Settings area, choose a file format. For this example, because we are optimizing a photo, choose JPEG. (You could choose PNG, but this format is not as widely accepted yet. Photos are best represented in JPEG because it can display the full range of color values. The GIF file format works better for line art that does not use the continuous-tone color transitions that photos rely on for a realistic portrayal of the universe around us.)

4. Below the file format setting is the quality level setting, which determines how much the file will be compressed. Start by choosing Medium, as this works best for most instances.

5. Notice the annotation under the right preview, just below the format type (JPEG). This information displays the compressed file size and approximate load time over a 56 Kbps connection. Right-click the preview image to change the modem speed if you want to optimize for slower or faster connections.

6. Adjust the quality levels until you achieve the optimum quality and load time. The name of the game is to get the lowest file size without overly sacrificing quality. Keep the view in 2-up mode (that is, both preview windows visible) so that you can visually compare the optimized version of the file with the original. You'll instantly know when you've compressed the file too much to give you a level of quality you can accept as adequate to your purposes. When you get to that point, move back up to the next highest level of quality.

7. When you are satisfied with the optimization, click OK and save the file.

89. E-mail Your Photos

E-mail—electronic mail—has become one the most common ways to send messages today. E-mail works through your Internet Service Provider (ISP) and the browser on your computer (plus whatever e-mail software programs you may be using). You can send your correspondence to anyone else in the world who has an e-mail address.

Why Would I Need to E-mail Photos?

One of the great attractions of e-mail, in addition to it being instantaneous (and not needing postage), is that you can attach many types of files to your message. You can attach image files as well as animation files. (Just be aware that many ISPs have limits on the size of an attachment.) You can send photos with your e-mail, which means that you need to convince all your relatives to get an e-mail account! With the proliferation of fast connections, fast computers, and high-quality printers, using e-mail to distribute images is becoming very practical.

How Do I Prepare and Send Photos by E-mail?

Sending images by e-mail creates the same challenges you encounter in displaying them on Web sites. E-mail uses the same phone (or cable) lines used by the Web and is limited by the connection speeds of individual systems. If you simply intend to display your image on the recipient's screen, you can optimize the image, as described in the previous tip. If you are sending a file to a print service bureau or publisher, you'll want the resolution to be high. But transferring a high-resolution image can be excruciatingly slow using a standard 56KB modem.

NOTE *Many e-mail providers place limitations on the file size of attachments. If the file is larger than 1MB, you may need to post it to an FTP connection instead of sending it via e-mail.*

The most popular e-mail programs allow you to send images with electronic messages in two ways: you can attach the file to the e-mail or you can insert the file in the body of the e-mail (as shown in Figure 13-2). If you attach the image, only its file name is displayed. To open or save the attachment, the recipient must usually double-click the file name. When you insert the file in the body of the e-mail, the image displays when the recipient opens the e-mail. You use an Attach button or Insert menu commands to perform these operations, depending on the e-mail software you are using.

Photoshop Elements has a convenient automated e-mail attachment program that can be accessed from the File menu. It prompts you to maintain the current size or automatically optimize.

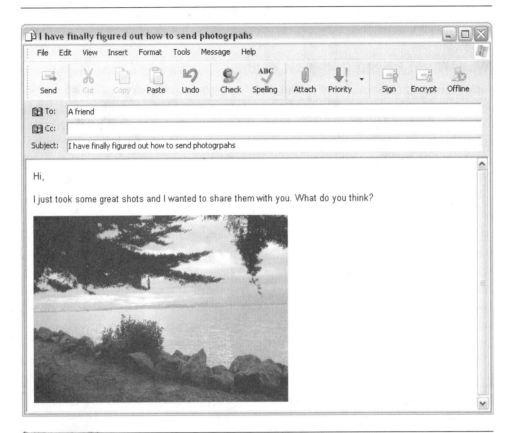

FIGURE 13-2   A photograph inserted in an e-mail

90. Turn Still Photos into Web Animation

Web animation is created in a file format called Graphics Interchange Format (GIF). Using GIF, you can stack multiple images of the same size into one file to display them sequentially in a browser—banner ads on Web pages commonly make use of animated GIF files. Because GIF files display a maximum of 256 colors, the images need to be converted from the format the camera produces. (This is discussed shortly.)

Why Would I Use Photos to Create Animation for the Web?

Digital cameras can capture time sequences of motion (see Tips 18 and 19 in Chapter 3) that can be displayed in an animated GIF format. You can adjust the time interval between the display of each frame in a GIF file if you're going for a slideshow look rather than a movie-type animation. You can present your images in any sequence, to make them instructive, provocative, or just for fun.

How Do I Take a Series of Photos and Create an Animation?

The tools for creating GIF animations are also included in the Save For Web dialog box (shown earlier in this chapter in Figure 13-1). Photoshop Elements makes setting up GIF animation easy by using the Layers Palette as a staging area. Each layer becomes an animation cell.

1. Start with a number of images stacked on separate layers. For best results, they should have the same dimensions.

2. Organize your layers so that the first image you want displayed is on the bottom and the last image is on the top.

3. Preview the transition between any two frames by making the upper frame invisible and then visible again.

NOTE   *If you are adding hand-drawn aspects, you can use the opacity value to make the upper layer partially transparent so you can see its relationship to the lower frame.*

4. After you have set up the layers, choose File | Save For Web (see Figure 13-3). This time, we will focus on the Settings and Animation sections.

5. Choose the GIF file format under Settings. Set the color quality to Adaptive. This causes Elements to choose the best 256 colors for display based on the original colors of the images.

6. While in the GIF optimization dialog, from the Dither drop-down menu, choose Diffusion (100 percent). Dithers create color patterns to simulate colors that are not available. Diffusion works best with photographic images. Select 256 from the Colors drop-down menu. This will let the file be optimized with the maximum amount of colors available for a GIF file.

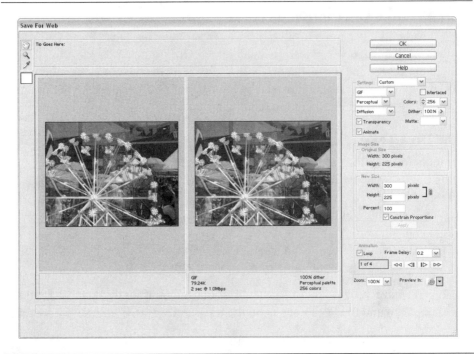

FIGURE 13-3   The Save for Web dialog box with GIF animation options

7. Check the Animate option in the Settings area, which becomes available only after you choose the GIF format. This will enable the Animation section at the bottom of the dialog box. You use these controls to set up the parameters for the animation.

8. Advance through each frame of the animation and make sure it is correct. Use the Frame Delay setting to control the time interval between frames.

9. If you want the animation to play continuously, check the Loop option.

10. Preview the animation in your browser.

11. When you are satisfied, click OK and save the file.

NOTE   *When you stack images in a GIF animation file, the size of the file grows accordingly. It's good practice to make GIF animations small in size or they may not load or play properly on the Web. Banner ads are a fairly typical measure of the maximum size of a GIF animation.*

91. Make an Instant Web Portfolio with Elements

You've set up your new Web site, and you're wondering how to get your photos displayed on the site in a good interactive fashion. Now that you know how to optimize your photos, you will learn how to get them onto a Web page by creating a Web *portfolio*. A portfolio provides you with a thumbnail menu of all your works. When you click a thumbnail, you see an enlarged version of that photo (or any other scanned artwork you care to display).

Photoshop Elements, and other software programs, provide automated routines that make putting together portfolios (or scrapbooks or catalogs) for the Web as simple as a few clicks. All the code, thumbnails, and images are placed automatically after you specify the style template, image and text sizes, and other options that seem most suited to your purpose. Photoshop Elements and many other programs come with style templates that provide a variety of theme interfaces.

Why Should I Use a Portfolio?

Creating from scratch an interactive album or portfolio on Web pages is a laborious job, and updating it is difficult, too. Unless you really need a custom design, you can use automated software to put together a decent portfolio. Not only does it take time and resources to learn to do your own Web page production, but you also need specialized software to develop Web pages. Another big plus with automated portfolios is that updating is a breeze. This will encourage you to post your work more often.

How Do I Create a Web Portfolio?

Photoshop Elements provides a nice routine for portfolio development called the Web Photo Gallery.

You will be surprised at how much work this program does in a short period of time. Building a Web portfolio from scratch can take you hours—or even days. Building such a portfolio in one of the programs that does it automatically takes only a few minutes … maybe half an hour, if you're really a picky person.

NOTE

As soon as you create a portfolio in Photoshop Elements, you can see, read, and modify the HTML that makes up the page. If you already have even a cursory knowledge of HTML, you can then do anything you'd like to modify the portfolio and can easily change the backgrounds, headline banners, and other styling touches to make it your own.

1. Create a new folder in your operating system's Explorer or Finder and give it a name that reminds you of its purpose (for example, Web Portfolio Images). Place all of the images you want to use in this specific portfolio into that folder. There is no need to resize or optimize these images—Photoshop Elements automatically does all that tedium for you.

2. Choose File | Create Web Photo Gallery to open the Web Photo Gallery dialog box shown in Figure 13-4.

3. Choose a style from the drop-down menu at the top of the dialog box. A thumbnail of the style will appear in the preview window on the right.

4. In the Folders area, click the Browse button and navigate to the source folder in which you placed all your images.

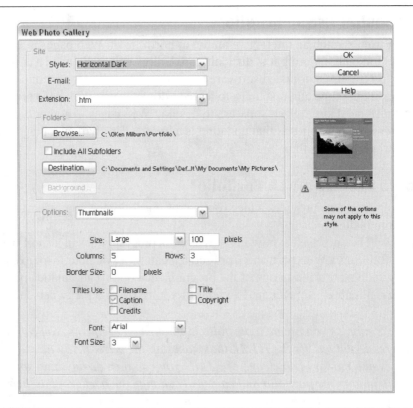

FIGURE 13-4   The Web Photo Gallery dialog box

5. Click Destination to select the path and folder where all the Web files will be stored. The program will then create a number of subfolders in which to store the different categories of files it has created for the portfolio site: large images, thumbnails, and Web pages. This makes it easy to find and modify them once the site has been generated.

6. In the Options area of the Web Photo Gallery dialog, you will find a pull-down menu that will bring up separate options dialogs for each of the following: Banner, Large Images, Thumbnails, Custom Colors, and Security. The banner (should you choose to use one) is the heading you want to appear on all your gallery pages. Large images are the images that display after you click the thumbnails. You can set their size, optimization, and captions. Thumbnails are the small images that help the viewer of the portfolio navigate to the larger images. You can set their size and location (top, bottom, or side of the page—or on a separate Web page as a "contact sheet"). Vertical row or column thumbnail styles will automatically scroll the thumbnails if there are more of them than will fit on one screen. The Custom Colors option sets the colors of the text and hyperlinks. Security defines the information you want listed with the images, such as copyright and credits.

7. When you are through setting the parameters, click OK.

8. The program opens, optimizes, and saves each image in sequence. The program is also creating Web pages, thumbnails, and all the code to make the gallery function on the Web. Figure 13-5 shows the finished Web gallery page.

9. Copy the file directory structure on your Web host server, and your gallery is ready for prime time. Contact your Web hosting service for specific instructions about uploading your files.

92. Caption and Frame Web Photos

Captioning is the process of placing a title or descriptive text next to the photograph or inside a border. *Framing* is the process of applying a decorative border to an image. You can create many types of frames by hand, or you can use some of the automated features for framing images found on the Layer Styles Palette.

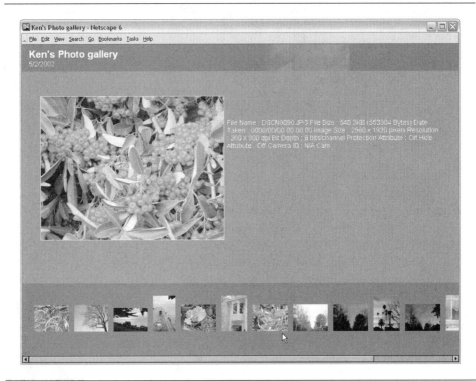

The completed Web gallery page

Why Would I Want to Frame and Caption Images?

Framing a digital image is much like framing a piece of art. It provides a visual separation from the background environment and keeps the viewer's focus within the work. If the background color for your Web page is similar to that of your photographs, a frame will help set off your pictures. Borders, such as torn edges, can also add a stylized look to the image.

Captions are used mostly to provide information to the viewer. Captions can provide the file name, photo title, artist name, copyright, date, size, price, type of camera, settings, a description of where or how the shot was taken, identities of the people in the shot, personal thoughts, and pretty much any information you want to convey.

How Do I Frame and Caption Web Photos?

Captions are applied with the Text tool in the Toolbox (see Tip 87 in Chapter 12). As you can see in Figure 13-6, text can be applied in a number of different ways and in different positions.

FIGURE 13-6 Photograph with stylized border and a number of caption types

Here's how to apply text to a caption:

1. Choose the Text tool from the Toolbox and click anywhere in the image to start typing the text. Type in the text.

2. Adjust the text style, color, and size in the Options bar. You can also move the text by dragging it to another part of the page.

Here's how to apply the annotation circle and line:

1. From the Toolbox, choose the Elliptical Marquee tool. Hold down the SHIFT key while making the selection to draw a perfect circle.

2. Choose the Pencil tool from the Toolbox. Hold down the SHIFT key while drawing the line to constrain it to a horizontal line.

3. Choose Edit | Stroke. The Stroke dialog box will appear. Set the width at 5 pixels and the color to white (or whatever color shows distinctly over your image). Location should be Center, blend mode Normal, and Opacity 100%.

Here's how to apply the black border:

1. Choose Image | Resize | Canvas Size. The Canvas Size dialog box will appear. Select the Relative option.

2. Type **200** in both the Width and Height fields. This will create a black border of 100 pixels wide on all sides.

Here's how to apply the frame:

1. From the Palette well, open the Effects Palette. Make sure All is selected in the drop-down menu.

2. Find the Brushed Aluminum effect. Drag it over the image. The program will run through a few automated routines and then apply the frame.

Try This: **Captioning for Copy Protection**

If you are concerned about people downloading your photographs and making copies without your permission, you can use captioning to prevent that. You can superimpose translucent copyright text over part of the image, which will discourage unauthorized use. It is not the most elegant solution, but it can help to discourage image piracy. There are also numerous watermarking programs sold for this purpose. Watermarks can be embedded invisibly and can be extracted even from images that have been cropped and edited.

Chapter 14

Printing Pictures that Look Good and Last

Now that you know how to get images into the camera, onto memory cards, out of the camera, onto your computer, and up on the Web, you need to learn some important issues about printing a digital image. One of the most significant changes to the digital imaging world is the advent of high-resolution color printing that can produce photo-quality output at an affordable price. These new printers give you a much higher degree of control over how, when, and where your prints are created. The world of digital printing is continuing to change dramatically and getting better all the time. Finally, the creation of photographs is totally in your hands.

93. Choose the Right Printer, Paper, and Ink

The plethora of printers, paper types, and ink types you'll find available at an office supply store or computer discount retailer can be daunting. When you're looking at a bank of 20 printers for sale, it might seem impossible to choose the right one without taking it home and trying it out. Short of that, you'll do yourself a favor by reading up on the various types of printers that are out there today to find out what services they offer and how they might fit your needs. The following information provides a primer to help you start out in the right direction.

What Kinds of Printers Are Available?

A number of printer technologies can be used to produce digital prints: inkjet, thermal-wax transfer, dye sublimation, laser, and film recorder printers. These are described in the following sections.

Of all these choices, the inkjet stands out as the most practical choice for the average photographer who wants to print photos. Desktop inkjet printers have moved to the forefront as the printer of choice, and for good reason. Inkjet printers deliver excellent quality and ease of use for an exceptionally low price. With the advances in inkjet technology, the prints can rival the quality of conventional photographic prints. The high cost of supplies has been an issue, but the proliferation of other manufacturers of paper and ink continues to bring prices down.

Inkjet Printers   Inkjets are inexpensive and versatile, and they produce good-quality prints. Inkjets spray a dithered pattern of microscopic ink dots on the paper to produce a printed image. They can print on a variety of materials, such as art papers, canvases, T-shirts, and ceramic transfer materials—even mouse pads. Inkjet printers are the leading printers used by consumers at this writing.

NOTE   *Inkjet printers, thanks to a great deal of pioneering work by Epson (and more recently Canon and Hewlett-Packard), have begun to be capable of producing prints of both long life (surpassing a type-C photographic print) and archival quality. If you plan on exhibiting and selling your digital photographs, it is imperative that you use such a printer. Ordinary inkjet prints will last for only a few months to a year.*

Thermal-Wax Printers   These high-quality printers transfer wax-based ink onto specially treated paper. They are used for photographic proofing and technical printing. Thermal printers are a bit more expensive than inkjets, and supplies are not as readily available. In general, they can match the quality of inkjet, but they are not as versatile.

Dye Sublimation Printers   These printers are capable of producing prints that are nearly indistinguishable from photographic prints, and they have a comparable life span. They produce rich color with no perceptible grain and are limited to tabloid and smaller print sizes. Used by professionals for color proofing, these printers and supplies are relatively expensive. This technology is used in a number of snapshot printers, but the cost per print is higher than standard photo prints.

Laser Printers   Laser printers are mostly used for high-speed, high-resolution, black-and-white printing. Color laser technology is very expensive and does not match the quality of any of the other print technologies.

Film Recorders   Film recorders transfer digital images to either positive or negative photographic film at very high resolutions. The slides are used for slideshows and the negatives can be printed by conventional means. Film recorders are commonly used for business graphics and cinematic frames.

Why Do I Need to Use Special Paper and Ink?

The quality and type of paper you use to print your images can make a world of difference, sometimes more than the printer itself does. Photo-quality, coated printing paper can be purchased at most office supply and photography stores. On some photo-quality inkjet printers, if you use regular paper to print your photographs, you'll get a soggy print without a lot of definition.

Inks, like paper, are not all created equal. Using quality, well-tested inks is also important to the performance of your printer.

Special Paper   Printer paper comes in all shapes, sizes, and types. You should use paper that has been specially treated for photographic printing on an inkjet printer. Look for papers that are clearly labeled for use with inkjet printers.

The surface quality, density, and texture of the paper determine how the ink takes to the surface. Whiteness, resistance to moisture distortion, and longevity are also important considerations. Thicker papers and papers with more rag content (the amount of cloth versus wood pulp content in the paper) will take large amounts of ink without distorting or wrinkling. Some papers are absorbent, which diffuses the color, while others keep the ink on the surface to allow for crisper detail. Each paper will affect how the color looks and can change the actual color of the print, often drastically.

If you are printing text and simple graphics, you can use a less expensive paper, because the demands on the coverage of ink are much less. On the other hand, if you are printing larger, complex color images like photographs, you will need paper that is stable (acid free), that is coated so that it can hold the minute detail, and that is white enough to provide clear, saturated color. You can get that kind of quality only by using the more expensive papers that are designed expressly for printing photographs.

Special Ink   Inkjet printers can use a number of types of inks, depending on your intended final product. Dye-based inks (most common because of their ability to produce a wider range of brightness) are chemically derived, pigment-based inks that use natural pigments like artist paints (longest lasting, but compatible only with very specific printers), and hybrid inks that combine both and are compatible with a somewhat wider range of printers. Hybrid inks are the latest generation of inks and are designed to optimize printer performance while also offering permanent color. (See Tip 97 later in this chapter for more on archival inks.)

The print head nozzle openings in an inkjet printer are microscopically small, so the ink needs to be very refined to pass through without clogging the nozzles. Color concentration and accuracy are also important to the color quality of the final print. You want ink that is going to be consistent from one cartridge to another. The final color result is always going to be a combination of the inks and the paper you print on. Each printer manufacturer calibrates its printers to a particular ink standard, so you need to use ink that is approved for use with your printer.

> NOTE   *Inkjet printers use a variety of ink cartridges that can change with every brand and model. You must use the appropriate type of cartridge for your printer, so make sure you have printer model and/or cartridge model number handy when you want to purchase new ink cartridges.*

How Do I Select the Right Papers?

Selecting the right paper can be a confusing task if you don't know what you need and what's available. When in doubt, carefully read the manufacturer's recommendations included in your printer's manual. Also, be aware that changing papers requires a change in printer profiles if you expect to maintain color accuracy. When you find a paper you like, stick with it so you won't have to adjust your print settings each time you use a new brand of paper.

Papers come in varying textures and thickness. The thickness of paper is often stated in pounds. This term comes from how much a ream (500 sheets) of paper weighs. You'll find a paper weight number on the package. One might guess that the higher the number, the thicker the paper will be. However, the density of the paper stock plays as much a factor as its thickness, so different types of paper can give the same weight rating even though the thickness varies. The best bet is to ask the paper vendor to let you test a sample if you are unsure.

Following are some general categories you can use as guidelines when looking for the right paper for your printing needs.

Plain Paper   This is the standard type of paper you would use in any copier or fax. It is not treated in any special way for inkjet printing and absorbs ink at a fairly high rate, so it will wrinkle (and get soggy) if you print large, solid areas of color. Even if you're only printing text, the edges of the type will be fuzzy. When you set your printer parameters, choosing plain paper will cut back on the ink flow to help compensate. Plain paper will not produce quality color printing and should be used only for proofing text and simple line graphics printing.

Coated Paper   Coated paper is designed to work with inkjet printers. If it says "inkjet paper" on the package, you know that it is coated with a special kind of clay compound that reduces the ink absorbency and allows the colors to stay on the surface without polluting one another. The result is a richer print. Even with this coating, letter-weight office papers are still not good for printing images that have large areas of color. Coated paper is good for printing brochures, flyers, and other illustrated documents, but it is not optimal for pure photographic prints. It is, however, a good low-cost solution for testing positioning and size before printing the final image on higher-quality paper. Remember, though, color proofing isn't worth much if it's not done on the same paper on which you'll make the final print.

Photo Paper   Photo paper is also coated, but the coating is much heavier. It comes in glossy, semigloss, and matte finishes. Photo paper is of a much higher quality than regular coated paper and is processed to have a whiter appearance, so printed colors are more accurate. Paper with more rag content will tend to stay whiter longer and doesn't deteriorate with age as quickly. This is a good choice for printing home photographs.

NOTE   *Make sure you print on the coated side of the photo paper. If you print on the wrong side, you'll get nothing but a gooey, inky mess.*

Premium Photo Paper   This glossy, semigloss, and matte photo paper is the highest-quality paper you can use for digital photographic prints. These papers tend to be heavier stock and therefore more stable (and more expensive). The printed colors will appear rich, and the prints will have the same finish you get from standard photographic print processing. Premium acid-free papers are designed to last and maintain color for the longest period of time. These papers are pricey, so use them for prints you plan to keep.

NOTE   *If you really want prints that last long enough to be sold and collected, read the upcoming Tip 97 on archival printing.*

Other Materials   Since the advent of inkjet printers, paper manufacturers have scrambled to deliver all sorts of specialty printing substrates. You can buy a wide array of materials, including canvas, linen, plastic film, and watercolor paper—to name a few. You can also find specialty papers to use for specific print projects, such as calendars, cards, and labels. Remember that each new paper or material will take ink differently, so you will need to test them and adjust your print settings to get the best print.

How Do I Select the Right Ink?

If you use the inks that are recommended by the printer manufacturer, you can't go wrong. These inks are not always the cheapest, but they are the safest bet in terms of printer performance and image quality. If you do a lot of printing, the cost of ink cartridges can start to outpace the price you paid for the printer. In answer to these high costs, some ink manufacturers have started making ink that is marketed to be replacement alternatives to the name-brand inks.

NOTE   *The quality of these second-party inks can vary. Be careful when changing ink cartridge brands, because they can sometimes react with the ink already in the system and cause clogging. It is a good idea to flush your printer before changing to a new brand of ink. Cleaning kits are available for this purpose. Also, bargain inks of low quality may damage your printer—especially if your printer prints more than 1200 DPI or more than four colors. Be sure you've done your research before you buy such inks ... or at least have a friend who has the same printer as yours and can report a positive experience.*

94. Create and Print Projects

A *project* is the process of printing layouts on special-purpose materials. Some examples of "projects" would be greeting cards, mouse pads, coffee cups, aprons, scrapbooks, portfolios, invitations, announcements, calendars, newsletters, labels, postcards, brochures, business cards, and most other common layouts into which you can place a photo.

A number of products on the market provide a library of print projects for you to work with. You don't need to be experienced with graphic design or layout to put together a nice project. When it comes to special materials, such as coffee cups, there are many online services that will both acquire and print them for you. The automated process used in these products is designed to walk you step-by-step through building a project, making it easy for the amateur to accomplish fairly complex layouts.

Microsoft Picture It! (Figure 14-1) is an inexpensive and easy-to-use application that features extensive project libraries which make it very easy to incorporate your photos into the appropriate special-purpose layout. Other programs provide good project templates, including Canon Home Addition, Adobe PhotoDeluxe, ArcSoft PhotoStudio 2000 (one of the few that works on either Mac or Windows), and Ulead Photo Express 4.0. Most of these programs sell for less than $50 or can be had as part of the purchase of a product such as a camera, printer, or scanner. At those prices, you can afford to build a collection of them. Most of these programs also have other capabilities, such as panoramic stitching or mosaic photos.

Why Would I Need to Create a Project?

After you have taken some great photos, you may want to include them in a publication, such as an invitation or maybe a calendar. You could choose to take your photos to a print shop and have them lay it out for you, but that is complicated and expensive.

Print projects can help. Print projects automate the process by providing a modifiable predesigned layout and then walking you through the all the steps necessary to produce that project. Using print projects, you can use your photo collection to develop many practical printed pieces, transforming your home photo studio into an in-house publishing enterprise.

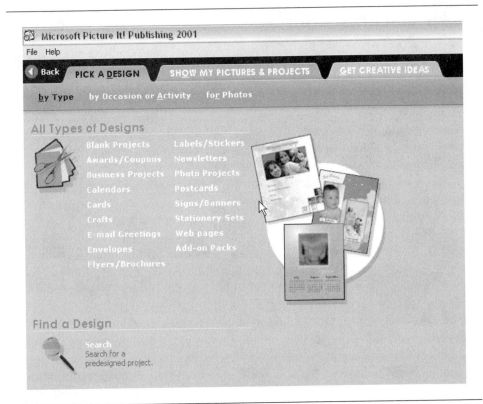

FIGURE 14-1   Microsoft's Picture It! Publisher 2001

How Do I Go About Printing a Project?

Because every print project application approaches this process a bit differently, the following procedure provides a general idea of the kind of things you can do with print projects software.

1. Decide what kind of project you want to lay out. The program will provide you with a list of categories. Choose one.

2. Within the category will be a range of templates, which were laid out by top-notch graphic designers, to give you a creative range of choices (as shown in Figure 14-2). These designers have made some preset choices about the decorative components of each theme. Pick a theme you like—or if you don't like what you see, you can modify one or start with a blank template.

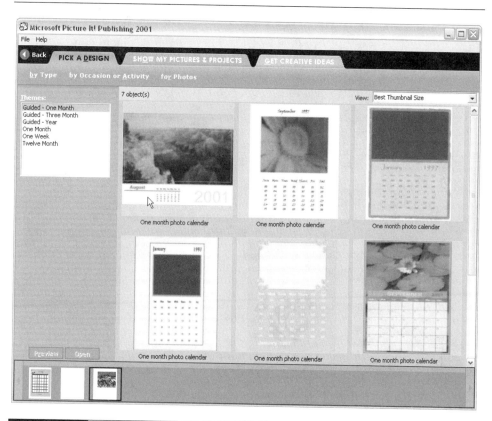

FIGURE 14-2   Some sample templates for Microsoft Picture It!

3. Next you have the option of accepting what has been provided or changing or modifying any of the components.

4. Adjust the sizes and shapes of the project's components (such as photos, headlines, and copy), as necessary.

5. Browse, select, and add your photos to the template. You can edit them in the process if necessary.

6. Type in and edit the copy.

7. Save or print the project.

It is really that simple. The help functions in these programs are extensive, so you will have plenty of help along the way.

95. Calculate Resolution Needed for Printed Publication

You will see the terms DPI (dots per inch) and PPI (pixels per inch) commonly used in relation to resolution. PPI is often referred to as *pixel resolution* and always refers to the pixel dimensions of the image. DPI refers to the *printer resolution*, which is always three times the PPI resolution.

Chapter 1 covered pixel resolution of the camera and digital-image files. This section focuses on resolution as it applies to printers.

Because printer resolution is a bit different than image resolution, you need to do some conversion to equate the two. All printers produce color using four colors: cyan, magenta, yellow, and black. The printer creates all the colors you see by placing individual dots of each of these four colors over or next to each other. This is similar to the way color in magazines is created. For every color pixel in the image, the printer has to put down three dots of color (black is not counted because it only determines how dark a color will be). So, ideally, you want the image size to contain one-third the number of pixels that the printer prints at its lowest resolution.

When you print at higher resolutions, most (usually, all) of the extra dots are derived from the image's base resolution—that is to say, they are *interpolated*. So having more than one-third of the printer's base resolution won't do you much good.

Why Do I Need to Calculate Resolution?

There is no benefit to having more resolution in an image than the printer can handle effectively. Extra resolution will just increase the size of the file, take up space on your hard disk, slow down the printing process, and cost you lots of extra money for ink. Calculating the correct resolution you will need allows you to size your project to be the most efficient. It also tells you if you do not have enough resolution for maximum image definition. Printing an image with less resolution than is required will force the printer to interpolate the image to the minimum size necessary to match the output size, in inches, that you specified. Interpolation will soften the image. Matching the required resolution of the printer with the actual resolution of the image file will give you the sharpest print.

You should also understand how printers are rated in terms of resolution. The *base* resolution is the lowest resolution rating; this is the actual resolution of the printer. Any higher resolution than the base resolution is interpolated and does not actually increase detail—it just increases the apparent smoothness of the transition between dots (because there are more of them, crowded more closely together). Printing at higher resolution also puts more ink on the paper and this can have the effect of making the colors appear to be more intense. It's a little like using thicker oil paints.

How Do I Calculate Print Resolution for My Project?

The easiest way to think about calculating printer resolution is to understand that the image resolution in PPI should be one-third of the printer resolution in DPI. For example, if a printer has a base rating of 720 DPI, it can place 720 distinct color dots per inch of output on the paper. Because it takes three dots to realize one pixel, the print resolution will need to be 720 / 3 = 240 PPI. If the printer resolution is 720 DPI, the PPI will need to be 240 (720 / 3 = 240).

NOTE   *The dot and the pixel are not equivalent. A dot represents a single micro drop of ink. Inks come in only four colors, so a dot can be only one of those four colors. Pixels, on the other hand, can be any of 16 million colors. The combination of those color dots produces the millions of colors we see in pixels. These terms are often interchanged and misused.*

When you are sizing your image for print, pay attention to the dialog box that controls image size. In Photoshop Elements' Image Size dialog box the Resolution setting, in pixels per inch, needs to be set to match your printer's resolution using the method just described.

You determine the image resolution as it relates to the size of the final print in your program's Image Size command. The first thing you want to know is: How big a print can I make given the real pixel resolution of the image? To find out, open the Image Size command's dialog box (in Photoshop Elements, choose Image | Resize | Image Size). The first thing you do is turn off Image Resampling. Then enter the resolution you need for your printer in the Resolution field. The Image Size for your document will change immediately. This is the maximum size you can print that image without resampling. If that dimension is larger than you intend to make the actual print, you're in good shape. If not, you're going to lose some image definition. You will lose too much image definition if you have to print at a size that's more than twice that of the original. It's as simple as that.

NOTE   *It's a very good idea to set the image size to its maximum resolution when you save your file for archival purposes. Then you have a perfect starting point any time you're ready to make another print.*

96. Make Your Photos into Gifts

Photographs are a wonderful source to use for making all sorts of gifts. Many online services can apply digital photos to several products. MSN Photos, for example, shown in Figure 14-3, offers a number of options for photo gifts. By

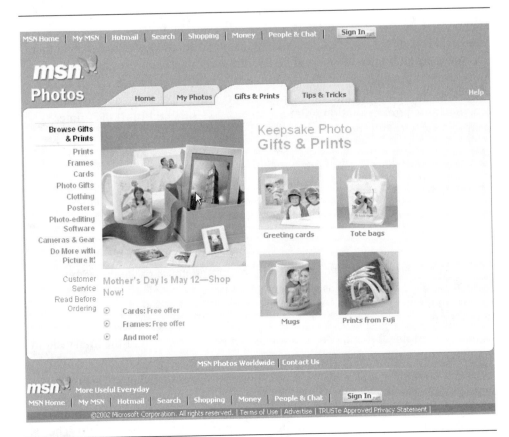

FIGURE 14-3   MSN Photos has a full line of gifts.

adding some text, you can personalize these gifts with names, dates, special messages, or sayings. You can create mugs, posters, T-shirts, cards, tote bags, puzzles, photo cubes, mouse pads, magnets, coasters, clocks, hats, key chains, and ties. Search the Web for "photo gifts" and you'll find many sites that offer these services. Kits for making most of these types of projects are available through such stationery manufacturers as Avery and many are available at your local office supply retailer, computer store chain, or online. However, it's often easier and cheaper to have such gifts made for you through an online resource, such as MSN Photos (http://photos.msn.com/).

A new-generation product called a *digital frame* is a unique item available from Digi-Frame, Nikon, Sony, and others. These frames are designed to look like typical picture frames, but the image area is a flat-panel display that can display any digital image. Imagine a framed photo that you can change as often as you like, just by slipping your camera's memory card into a slot on the frame. Some digital frames let you connect to the Internet through a phone line and download images from there, allowing you to network and send images to others.

Why Should I Create Personalized Gifts?

After you have captured digital images in your computer, you can turn them into true mementos by adding personal touches with your image editor. Take a photo of a birthday, wedding, new baby, pet, or graduation; add a personal message, name, memorable date, saying, or even poetry, and you can create a one-of-a-kind gift. If you run a small business, you can make promotional gifts by including a logo and contact information. All this can be done through the Web from the comfort of your home or business.

How Do I Use My Software and Printer to Make Gifts?

If you are using an online service, you will need to follow the instructions and provide any information the service requires to manufacture the products to your specifications. This can be as simple as uploading your digital photo and letting the service handle the rest; or you can do some magic in your image editor first. Most services require that your images conform to a certain resolution and file format, which you can easily create with your image editor. Add the text, frames, or any special effects you want and then save the file in TIF format, which is universally accepted. You will then need to upload your pictures to the Web service.

If you are more ambitious and you want to take over the whole process of creation, you can do a few things on your own. Some decal and iron-on materials can be used in your inkjet printer. You can then apply the decals or iron-on art to various items.

As mentioned previously, you can purchase special paper sets that are prepared for print projects such as calendars, greeting cards, and invitations. Use these in combination with project software to become your own print shop. The paper packages usually come with setup specifications, making it easy to configure the print area in your software to print them correctly.

> NOTE   *When you use these specialty paper packages, be aware that they don't supply extra paper for testing purposes. I always cut some cheap paper to the same size and perform printing tests on that paper so I don't waste any of the expensive stock. Even so, I often mess up a few. It's a good idea to buy some extra paper when you purchase these packages so you are not left short.*

97. Archive Printing Techniques

Archiving is a process of maintaining important documents, images, clippings, and other objects for posterity. An archival print is created in a way that maximizes its potential to stay in good condition for a long period of time, so it can be enjoyed in the future.

Archival prints have everything to do with the materials from which the prints are made. The digital information has no effect on it other than the fact that you are using digital printers to produce the print. The substrates, inks, dyes, and pigments all interact to determine how long the photographic image will last. Many of the materials used for digital printing are treated to make the ink, dyes, and pigments look better. The chemical interactions among paper, inks, and environmental conditions—such as light, humidity, and air pollution—can have dramatic effects, causing colors to fade and papers to yellow or disintegrate in a relatively short 2–24 months. With the advent of higher-resolution digital cameras, powerful desktop computers, and advanced image-editing software came a demand for printing technologies that would produce digital prints that were at least comparable to conventional photographic prints and, preferably, of archival museum quality. The result is that with some careful shopping for all the right elements, it is now possible to make digital photographic prints that are rated to last longer than any traditional artistic medium. At this writing, such printers costing less than $2000 are made only by Epson.

Within the last few years, printer manufacturers have developed papers and inks that met the standard and went beyond it for prints that are considered archival quality. The most important development to make this a reality came in the form of pigmented inks. These inks are formulated from raw pigment, not from chemical dyes like earlier inks. Pigments are much more stable and will not break down in light and humidity as will many chemical dyes.

Why Do I Need to Create Archival Quality Prints?

Some prints are not meant or made to last—such as magazines, posters, or food labels, for instance. Other types of images, however, are more important, and it is desirable that they last through many years, or even generations—think of family photos, art, and historic pictures. When you are printing photos that you want to last, it is important that you understand how to make them archival prints so those who view them decades later can enjoy seeing what your world looked like. If your photographic interests become more serious, you can make your digital prints collectible. This demands that you print with archival methods.

NOTE *Remember that the digital photos themselves, as long as they are stored on media that remains stable or doesn't become demagnetized, will never deteriorate. As long as the data is intact, you will be able to reproduce a digital image with perfect fidelity in 10,000 years. So just because you have already made prints with short life spans doesn't mean you can't make better ones as the technology continues to improve.*

How Do I Create Archival Prints?

If you want your prints to last more than 50 years, and in some cases more than 100 years, you will need to use some form of pigmented inks. Epson is one of the leaders in developing pigmented inks for its line of desktop inkjet printers. The company succeeded in developing inks that work with select printers like the P2000. New pigmented ink, called Generations Enhanced Micro-Bright Pigmented Inks, is being marketed through http://www.Inkjetmall.com and http://www.Inkjetart.com. This ink is rated at 100-years-plus and will work in most of the Epson inkjet printers.

NOTE *Each of the sites mentioned above is a great place to learn more about archival inks, papers, and advanced printing in general.*

If you want long-lasting prints, your choice of printing papers and other substrates is just as important as your choice of inks. No sense putting inks that will last 100 years on paper that will fall apart in 5. Premium photo papers are acid and oxidant free, which means that when the paper was manufactured, certain chemicals were not used in processing the paper, eliminating acidic residue in the fiber. Acid content can react with sunlight, air, and inks to cause deterioration. Archival papers are made from 100 percent rag (cloth fiber) and will stay whiter and hold together much longer than other papers made from a mixture of rag and pulp.

The last option is to go to print service bureaus that use professional-level printers and inks to provide superb color and archival prints. Search under "Giclée printing" (the name for high-end inkjet printing) to find a printer near you. This is an expensive solution, but it might be worth it for a treasure you want to display and keep for a long time.

There are also very expensive (mostly in the quarter million–dollar range) photographic printers that use lasers to print a digital image on photographic papers (the longest lasting is Fuji Crystal Archive). The Durst Lambda and Cymbolic Sciences Lightjet are the printers in this category to look for. You have to see a print made by one of these printers to realize how stunning it can be. If you need ultimate detail and photographic quality in your landscapes and studio still-lifes (and you have clients who will pay for it), look for printing services that use these printers. The average cost will be between $8 and $16 per square foot.

98. Print Without a Computer

It is possible to print digital photographs directly from camera to printer, bypassing the computer. Some models of printers are equipped with special input adapters that accept direct printing from the camera, memory cards, or wireless communications.

Why Would I Want to Print Without a Computer?

If you need to produce prints at a remote location, this method can make that possible. Portable-size printers that print directly from the camera, such as the Canon Card Photo Printer CP-100, can print 4×6 dye sublimation prints for super high quality, and they work on batteries. This turns you into a walking photo studio. This setup is ideal, for example, at gatherings where you want to hand out (or sell) photos as you take them. This is as close as you can get to a Polaroid, except the quality is better, you can make duplicates, and you have a digital photo which you can edit and improve on once you're back at the computer.

How Do I Print Directly to the Printer?

You will need to purchase a printer that is fitted for direct printing. Printers like the HP Photo Direct 100 and the Epson Photo 895 come with memory card slots that allow you to insert your SmartMedia, CompactFlash, or PC Cards right into the printer and print directly from the card. Other printers also offer direct cable connections from the camera to the printer. The HP Photosmart 1215 color printer uses a system called "Beam and Print," which employs an infrared wireless connection (but of course, you have to use their camera).

99. Print Without a Printer (Online)

If you have an Internet connection and you want to make prints of your digital images, you can send your images to online service centers, where they can be processed and printed to your specifications.

Online photo centers work through Web sites. Some of the top sites can be found at http://www.ofoto.com (see Figure 14-4), http://www.snapfish.com, http://www.shutterfly.com, http://www.photopoint.com, http://www.zing.com, http://www.photonet.com, and http://www.photoworks.com.

Why Would I Want to Print Directly Online?

For those who do not want to get into image editors and desktop printers, the online printing solution is the answer. Getting photos printed correctly and consistently on your own printer can be tricky, especially for those who are not too familiar with computers. Online services offer an alternative that can make the task of getting prints a breeze.

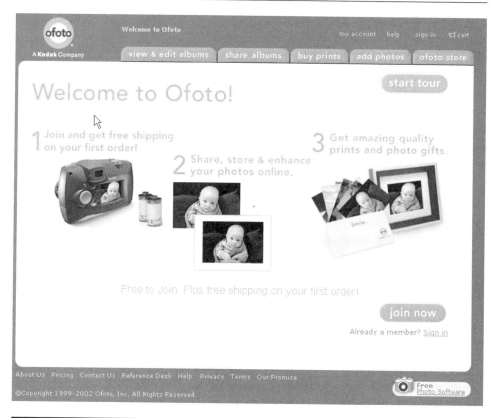

FIGURE 14-4   Ofoto is a typical online photographic service center offering albums, galleries, online editing, prints, and gifts.

How Do I Connect and Print Online?

To access this type of service, you open an account, upload your images to the site, and then indicate what you want. Based on your instructions, the company prints your images on high-end printers and mails the printouts to you. Most of these companies use automated interactive menus that allow you to indicate options and even edit your photos online if you want. You can designate a crop, reduce red eye, add borders, or enlarge the image. You can also indicate how many photos you want and the size you want them. They can mail or e-mail duplicates to other people as well.

Features, prices, and delivery times vary significantly from one service to another, so do some research first. One of the best ways to compare is to test each service with small orders. Make sure that you keep duplicates of the files you send, in case the company loses them. Many of the online photo services also offer a variety of print projects and products, such as cards, albums, and framing options.

NOTE   *Many of the online services will allow you to put the photos on their site so that others can order prints for themselves. Beware of doing this if you plan to make any money from those photos. Nobody's likely to pay much for something that they can easily get for the price of a print.*

Chapter 15

Handy, Affordable Accessories

It's surprising how many small (and mostly affordable) pieces of additional hardware are available to help you solve problems. These items include everything from close-up lenses for extreme macros to bags that protect your camera in inclement weather. When I know of a way to help you create or improvise one of these gadgets, I've mentioned that, too.

Close-up Lenses

Close-up lenses are magnifying optics that screw or slip on to your camera's main lens. You can use a close-up lens to photograph a subject that is closer to the camera than the built-in lens's minimum focusing distance allows. These lenses are ideal for shooting *macro* (extreme close-up) photography. You probably would like a close-up lens if you love to examine small details in nature, such as a butterfly's eyes, or if you want to photograph a collection of small items such as postage stamps or seashells.

Using a Close-up Lens

How close will you have to be before you need a close-up lens? That's a tough question to answer because every camera's minimum focusing distance is different. It's best to look it up on your camera's specification sheet or in the manual. You'll usually see a minimum focusing distance listed there. Typically, digital cameras will focus down to about 18 inches without requiring an accessory lens. However, some will focus down to 2 or 3 inches. Some Nikon Coolpix-series cameras will focus down to less than 1 inch and are unlikely to ever need an add-on close-up lens.

Close-up lenses are rated in *diopters*. You can think of diopters as "degrees of magnification." A 1 diopter close-up lens will get you half again as close as not having a close-up lens. A 2 diopter close-up lens will get you another 50 percent closer than that, and so on. You get the picture (pun intended). The diopter numbers are handy references, because you can add diopters together to get the total number of diopters of magnification. So if you add a 1 diopter and a 3 diopter lens, you get 4 diopters.

To take pictures using a close-up lens adapter, you will need to keep the camera rock steady, because the slightest camera movement will be exaggerated in the shot. Using a tripod is a good idea. Frame your picture through the LCD viewfinder instead of the optical viewfinder eyepiece (unless you have a single-lens reflex, SLR, camera). Your optical viewfinder simply won't give you accurate framing, and *parallax error* (the difference between the position of the optical viewfinder and that of the picture-taking lens) will be more exaggerated as you move closer to your subject. In fact, in macro photos, your picture may hardly be in the viewfinder.

Extension Lenses

Extension lenses are larger, multiple-element (several stacked optics) lenses. Like close-up lenses, they screw or slip on to the front element of your camera's main lens. Extension lenses aren't used to move you physically closer to the subject, but to widen or narrow the camera's field of view. That's why they're generally called wide-angle or telephoto extension lenses. You can buy extension lenses that give you anything from a 180-degree fish-eye, to a 600mm (or longer) telephoto that gives you a mere 5-degree angle of view.

Extension lenses give your camera a wider (wide-angle) or narrower (telephoto) field of view than is normally possible within the zoom range of your camera's built-in lens. It is important that you precisely frame your pictures in the camera in digital photography—especially if you're using the more popular and affordable 2- and 3-megapixel cameras—because cropping the picture after the fact can result in unacceptable image detail and sharpness.

Using an Extension Lens

The mechanical techniques for using extension lenses are much the same as those for close-up lenses. Wide-angle extension lenses make camera movement blur less obvious, but telephoto extension lenses are likely to require the use of a tripod. You're also going to need to frame your pictures using the camera's LCD monitor, because the camera's built-in optical viewfinder can't broaden or narrow the frame beyond the limits of the built-in zoom lens.

Because extension lenses are heavier than close-up lenses and filters, cameras that allow them to be screwed on will be much less likely to have the picture go out of focus because the supplementary and primary lenses are too far apart. They also protect your investment by making it much less likely that your extension lens will fall off the camera and into the lake or onto the railroad tracks.

Filters

Filters are optically transparent materials that cover the lens. Filters come in three basic types—color balancing, special effects, and polarizing—and in a number of configurations. They may be round screw-on/slip-on glass or they may be gelatin that fits into frames. As accessories go, filters are fairly inexpensive. Most cost well under $50.

Color-Balancing Filters and Gels

Filters can be purchased for either black-and-white or color photography. Those that are made for correcting the color of light are most important to digital photographers.

Although your camera will balance for the color of light automatically, you will get less noisy (grainy) images if you balance indoor lighting for daylight. To change the color of indoor (incandescent) light to the color of daylight, simply buy an 81A filter at your local camera store that will fit into your camera's screw-in filter threads or into a slip-on adapter made for your camera. If you are shooting indoors with incandescent lights on stands, you can also find much less expensive 81A *gels* (sheets of gelatin) that you can hang in front of your lights.

You can easily re-create the effects produced by the color-balancing filters made for traditional black-and-white photography if you are shooting digitally. To do that, you either simply add the color of the filter to tint the image before converting it to black-and-white or use one of the color channels—whichever comes closest to the effect you are after.

Special-Effects Filters

Special-effects filters give a specific "look" or character to an image. Traditional film photos that you've most likely noticed as having been taken through a special-effects filter are those of old movie stars whose skin seems to glow or car ads in which every bright highlight seems to glisten like a little star. If your image-editing program is compatible with Adobe Photoshop plug-in filters, you can get much more versatility in the intensity and variables in effects from such third-party vendors as Andromeda and Corel's KPT series of digital filters.

Polarizing Filters

Polarizing filters are used to cut the excess reflection of light from reflective surfaces. Their principal use is to darken the skies in color photographs, to cut reflections from the surface of water, and to kill reflection from the glass covering framed artwork and documents. Polarizing filters are available as both glass accessory lenses and as gel sheets for polarizing studio lights.

You can polarize either the light entering the lens or the light sources themselves. Of course, the latter is possible only if you are in a controlled studio lighting situation. For most purposes, just ask for the least expensive circular polarizing filter that will fit your camera's lens.

To use a lens-mounting polarizing filter, view the picture you are going to take through the LCD monitor and turn the polarizing filter until you see the effect you want—then take the picture.

Tripods

Tripods, as most readers of this book are likely to encounter them, are three-legged telescoping camera stands that hold the camera rock steady when you are shooting at shutter speeds of less than 1/125 of a second (or shorter, if you're the jittery type). Tripods are also useful for holding the camera while you're doing something else, such as positioning a flash or holding a reflector.

Pictures taken in existing lighting conditions are, for the most part, more likely to reproduce what you saw and the emotions you felt when you were there. Provided the subject isn't moving rapidly, you can take pictures in next to no light. However, you'll have to keep your camera still as Mt. Rushmore. This is especially true of photos taken indoors in dim light and outdoors during twilight and evening hours.

Choosing the Right Tripod

Tripods come in all sizes, weights, and prices. Still, it's easier to choose the right one than the variety might make you think. The most important things to look for are quality components and good engineering. Nothing is more annoying than a tripod head that won't stay exactly where you positioned it.

In addition to quality, look for as much versatility as you can get for the money. The tripod should extend to at least 6 feet with the center post up, but you want it to collapse to as short a length as possible. You also want it to be as lightweight as possible, but still rigid when it's fully extended. It won't do you any good to own a tripod if you refuse to take it with you because it's too big. On the other hand, a tripod that gets wobbly in a strong breeze is next to useless.

When it comes to taking pictures in the sort of lighting conditions that require a tripod, you need to keep a few tips in mind. As lighting conditions dim, it's more likely that a few bright lights will mislead your camera's built-in meter. Take a few pictures, review them on your LCD screen, and then set your exposure manually to match the exposure of the best shots. If your camera has a bracketing mode, so much the better for taking the test shots. In addition, dim light exposures are often quite long, which increases the noise (grain) in the picture. If your camera has a noise reduction feature, use it.

Other Devices to Steady Your Camera

In addition to the tall, telescoping tripods, there are also table-top tripods. Many of these are too cheesy to be useful, but some excellent ones are available for under $30, and they'll fit neatly into your camera bag. Table-top tripods can be braced against almost any type of surface—even vertical walls and posts—so they're amazingly versatile.

Two other "gadgets" that are handy are C-clamps with ball heads (see Figure 15-1) for mounting the camera, and bean bags. C-clamps can be attached to tall ladders, tree branches, all sorts of railings, the edges of tables—the list goes on and on. Bean bags are great for irregularly shaped but steady surfaces, such as the hood of your car, a rock, or a fallen tree trunk. The camera stays steady because it can be nestled into the bag until it is level.

FIGURE 15-1   A ball head can be used on most tripods. Ball heads are comparatively inexpensive and adjust the camera to any angle with a single twist.

Cases

So many types, sizes, prices, and styles of camera cases are available that one could write a (very boring) book on the subject. However, you should keep a few tips in mind when considering a case for your digital camera and equipment:

- Is it big enough? Will it hold everything you want to have with you when you're shooting, especially the things you need most—a supplementary lens or two, an LCD hood, a table-top tripod, and an external flash? It's also nice if it's roomy enough to hold other personal belongings (checkbook, PDA, and so on), so you have to carry only one case.

- Is it strong enough? If you are going to check it as luggage, it should be made of some rigid material, such as plastic or aluminum. If it's going to stay on your person, it should be made of sturdy, bulletproof (read indestructible), and waterproof nylon.

- Is it padded? If it's made of nylon (such as a shoulder bag or backpack, as shown in Figure 15-2), be sure that it's foam padded. Then when it accidentally swings into a lamppost, your delicate digital camera may still be usable.

- Does it keep the camera dry and dust free in rainy or windy weather?

- How easy is it to steal? Like any really cool techno-gadget, digital cameras are favorite targets of thieves in airports, big cities, and vacation lands. At the very least, place the strap around your neck, and not just over your shoulder.

External Flash

If you like to shoot indoors, an external flash is the least expensive way to double the appeal of your photographs. External flashes come in a variety of sizes, shapes, powers, and prices. Some people make a whole sideline of their expertise in using external flash. Fact is, you can and should keep it both simple and affordable. Look for an external flash that has a built-in slave unit and that calculates exposure automatically—that way, you won't have to take the time to measure distances and figure out exposures. You also won't need to worry about physically connecting the external flash with your camera because it can be triggered by your camera's built-in flash, which will also provide fill light.

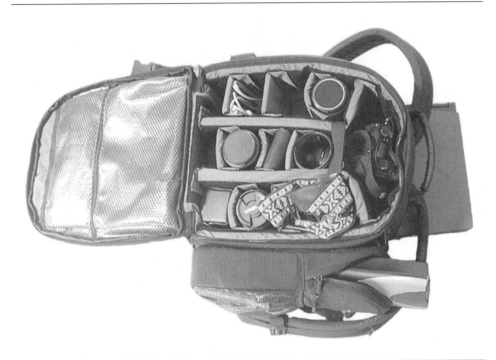

FIGURE 15-2   This backpack made for travel photography has room for several camera bodies and supplementary lenses, and even has space for carrying a laptop.

On the other hand, if your camera does provide a means of connecting to and synching with an external flash, you can turn off the built-in slave and operate the external flash that way. Such hard-wired synchronization lets you use the external flash when other photographers are present and using flash—and triggering your slave flash as a result. Hard-wired synchronization is also useful when you want to turn off your camera's built-in flash because you want deeper shadows than you'd get if the built-in flash were filling them.

Sunpak's external strobe, shown in Figure 15-3, is made especially for digital cameras, has a built-in slave unit, and can calculate exposures automatically. It also costs less than $50 in many stores.

FIGURE 15-3   Sunpak's external strobe

LCD Hoods

We could almost do without optical viewfinders if only LCD monitors could be seen clearly in lighting bright enough to permit handheld photography. On the other hand, if you're going to take carefully composed and framed digital photos, you want the previewing accuracy that you can only get from the LCD viewfinder. What to do, what to do? Simple: spend an extra 20 bucks and get a Hoodman LCD hood (http://www.hoodmanusa.com). It's a foldable nylon shade that attaches to your LCD monitor with Velcro strips or an elastic strap (better if you're borrowing someone else's camera) and makes your viewfinder viewable—even in bright sunlight. If you want to spend just a bit more, Screen-Shade (http://www.screen-shade.com) and Opt-X make somewhat fancier LCD shades that use a bellows to make them expand and contract. Or, if you really want to go the budget route, you can make your own LCD hood by cutting off the frosted plastic part of a slide viewer and holding it over the LCD. This is shown in Figure 15-4.

FIGURE 15-4   A homemade LCD hood

Be Prepared

You'll always need to carry a couple of extra items with you, although they aren't really "accessories" in the strictest sense of that word. You need extra digital "film" and camera batteries.

■ **Ken's Law**   You will always need to take the most important picture just after you've run out of space on your camera's memory card.

■ **Ken's Other Law**   Your camera will run out of power just before you need to take the most important shot and when you forgot extra batteries. (Battery chargers are also small enough that you can easily slip one into your camera bag.)

Index

Note: Page numbers in *italics* refer to illustrations or charts.

A

accessories, 245–255
    cases, 16–17, 251, *252*
    external flash, 251–252, *253*
    extra supplies, 255
    filters, 247–249
    LCD hoods, 253–254
    lenses, 246–247
    steadying cameras, 249–250
advanced techniques, 103–112
    animation, 110–112
    movies, 108–110
    panoramas, 104–108
Ambience slider, lighting effects, 200
animation, 110–112
    See also advanced techniques
    burst-mode series, 111
    GIF, 218–220
    object animation technique, 111
    overview, 110
    photographed sequences and,
      110–112
    slideshows, 112
aperture-priority mode, 38, 42–44
    See also automatic mode; shooting
      modes
    blur, 43, *44*
    depth-of-field, 42–43, *44*
    exposure times, 43
    focal length, 43
    how to use, 44

ISO ratings, 44
    overview, 42–43
archival printing, 240–242
    See also printing
archiving images via CD burners, 121,
    133–134
    See also managing photos
artwork. *See* documents and artwork;
    hand-drawn art and photos; vector art,
    text and photos
attachments, e-mailing photos, 217
audio mode. *See* video and audio modes
Auto Flash setting, built-in flash, 81
auto-bracketing, night shots and exposure
    settings, 100
autofocus, 64–65
    See also focus
automatic mode, 36–39
    See also digital cameras; shooting
      modes
    aperture-priority mode, 38
    overview, 36–38
    programmed mode, 37
    shutter-priority mode, 37–38
average center weighted metering, 72
    See also metering options

B

ball heads, tripods and, 250
batteries, 22–25
    changing or recharging, 24–25

INTERNATIONAL CONTACT INFORMATION

AUSTRALIA
McGraw-Hill Book Company Australia Pty. Ltd.
TEL +61-2-9417-9899
FAX +61-2-9417-5687
http://www.mcgraw-hill.com.au
books-it_sydney@mcgraw-hill.com

CANADA
McGraw-Hill Ryerson Ltd.
TEL +905-430-5000
FAX +905-430-5020
http://www.mcgrawhill.ca

**GREECE, MIDDLE EAST,
NORTHERN AFRICA**
McGraw-Hill Hellas
TEL +30-1-656-0990-3-4
FAX +30-1-654-5525

MEXICO (Also serving Latin America)
McGraw-Hill Interamericana Editores S.A. de C.V.
TEL +525-117-1583
FAX +525-117-1589
http://www.mcgraw-hill.com.mx
fernando_castellanos@mcgraw-hill.com

SINGAPORE (Serving Asia)
McGraw-Hill Book Company
TEL +65-863-1580
FAX +65-862-3354
http://www.mcgraw-hill.com.sg
mghasia@mcgraw-hill.com

SOUTH AFRICA
McGraw-Hill South Africa
TEL +27-11-622-7512
FAX +27-11-622-9045
robyn_swanepoel@mcgraw-hill.com

**UNITED KINGDOM & EUROPE
(Excluding Southern Europe)**
McGraw-Hill Education Europe
TEL +44-1-628-502500
FAX +44-1-628-770224
http://www.mcgraw-hill.co.uk
computing_neurope@mcgraw-hill.com

ALL OTHER INQUIRIES Contact:
Osborne/McGraw-Hill
TEL +1-510-549-6600
FAX +1-510-883-7600
http://www.osborne.com
omg_international@mcgraw-hill.com

New Offerings from Osborne's
How to Do Everything Series

How to Do Everything with Your Digital Camera
ISBN: 0-07-212772-4

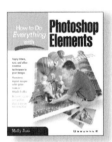

How to Do Everything with Photoshop Elements
ISBN: 0-07-219184-8

How to Do Everything with Photoshop 7
ISBN: 0-07-219554-1

How to Do Everything with Digital Video
ISBN: 0-07-219463-4

How to Do Everything with Your Scanner
ISBN: 0-07-219106-6

How to Do Everything with Your Palm™ Handheld,
2nd Edition
ISBN: 0-07-219100-7

HTDE with Your Pocket PC
2nd Edition
ISBN: 07-219414-6

How to Do Everything with iMovie
ISBN: 0-07-22226-7

How to Do Everything with Your iMac,
3rd Edition
ISBN: 0-07-213172-1

How to Do Everything with Your iPAQ
ISBN: 0-07-222333-2

OSBORNE
www.osborne.com

Orders: McGraw-Hill Customer Service 1-800-722-4726 fax 1-614-755-5645   For more information: Karolyn_Anderson@mcgraw-hill.com 1-617-472-3555   www.books@mcgraw-hill.com/library/html